THE Pittsburgh Steelers

Also by Ed Bouchette

Dawn of a New Steel Age

THE Pittsburgh Steelers

Ed Bouchette

ST. MARTIN'S PRESS NEW YORK

Editor: George Witte
Production Editor: Robert Cloud
Copyedited by Steven Miller

All photographs courtesy of the Pittsburgh Steelers

LIBRARY OF CONGRESS CATALOGING-IN-PUBLICATION DATA

Bouchette, Ed.
The Pittsburgh Steelers / Ed Bouchette.
p. cm.
ISBN 0-312-11325-0
1. Pittsburgh Steelers (Football team)—History. I. Title.
GV956.P57B68 1994
796.332'64'0974886—dc20 94-16792
CIP

First edition: September 1994
10 9 8 7 6 5 4 3 2 1

DEDICATION

Q. Which four people mean more than anything to me?
A. Debbie, Scott, Danielle, and Brittany.

ACKNOWLEDGMENTS

I could say all the questions, answers, facts, and figures that follow about the Pittsburgh Steelers came straight from my wealth of knowledge on the franchise. If that were true, this book might have been printed on the back of a cereal box.

Much of my research took place in the Art Rooney Library (remember this, you will be tested on it later) in the Steelers' offices at Three Rivers Stadium. Joe Gordon, the team's director of communications, helped point me in the right direction once I got there.

Others on the Steelers who provided facts or tidbits were President Dan Rooney, public relations coordinator Dan Edwards, former executive Jim Boston, and retired public relations director Ed Kiley, along with *Steelers Digest* editor Bob Labriola and retired *Pittsburgh Press* sports editor Pat Livingston. The Steelers also made available a treasure chest of photos.

My son, Scott, actually deserves more credit than what he's getting here. Some day when he writes his own book, he may remember that he did some work on this one. My wife, Debbie, also helped research many questions, but she told me she wanted no credit. So be it.

Thank you, all.

CONTENTS

Fourth Quarter

HAIL TO THE CHIEF

The phone rang early one morning while I was in Albuquerque, New Mexico, covering the Cleveland Browns' practices in the high altitude before their ill-fated AFC Championship game in Denver in 1987.

The Chief, Art Rooney Sr., was calling from Pittsburgh to chat.

"Albuquerque?" the Steelers' founder wondered. "You know, we played there once."

There may not be a big city in America in which Art Rooney's football teams did not play. In the old days, he would play anywhere if someone was willing to guarantee enough money to enable him to meet the payroll that week.

He once promised a friend to play an exhibition game in California in 1936 near the end of the season. Little did he know his ballclub would be in title contention then. The Pirates, as they were called at the time, took a train to play in Chicago November 15. They continued by train to Los Angeles for a November 22 game, then came all the way back across the country by train to Boston for a November 29 game against the Redskins. A victory in Boston would have put them in the playoffs. Exhausted from their travels, they lost 30-0.

Art Rooney, who died in 1988 at the age of 87, loved competition of any kind—the horses, football, baseball, boxing. He founded the Pittsburgh franchise in the National Football League in 1933, but he had owned and managed pro football and baseball teams long before that in Pittsburgh. If there was a sporting event of any kind in Pittsburgh, Art Rooney was interested. A new football field is named after him at Duquesne University. He promoted boxing matches and owned horse tracks. He was a fixture at Pirates baseball games almost to the day he died, and he knew their managers and many visiting National League managers because he would stroll up the hall from the Steelers' offices in Three Rivers Stadium to the baseball clubhouses—just to chat.

Art Rooney Sr.

Many of the anecdotes in the following pages came from Art Rooney. He and his football club have provided a history rich in them.

—Ed Bouchette

Kickoff

50 QUESTIONS

1 Who was Pittsburgh coach Bill Cowher's favorite Steeler while he was a teenager in Crafton, Pennsylvania?

•

2 Which quarterback started all three strike games for the Steelers in 1987?

•

3 Why did Hall of Fame linebacker Jack Lambert retire after the 1984 season?

a) He was cut
b) His teeth fell out
c) He had turf toe
d) He wanted to quit at the top of his game

•

4 In 1970, which team lost a coin flip with the Steelers for the right to make Terry Bradshaw the number one pick in the draft?

•

5 Who turned down the Steelers' coaching job in 1969 before they offered it to Chuck Noll?

a) Johnny Majors
b) Joe Paterno
c) Don Shula
d) Ara Parseghian

•

6 True or False: Joe Greene has more sacks than anyone in Steelers history.

•

7 What future Hall of Famer was benched temporarily by defensive coordinator Bud Carson during the 1974 AFC Championship?

•

8 Who did founder Art Rooney often say was his favorite Steeler?

•

9 Who were the only father and son to become Steelers assistant coaches?

•

10 How many head coaches did the Steelers have in 1941?

•

11 Which mother of a Steelers player competed for the title of Miss World?

•

12 Who was the Steelers' first $1 million-a-year player?

a) Bubby Brister
b) Rod Woodson
c) Terry Bradshaw
d) Louis Lipps

•

13 What was the Steelers' first playoff game?

a) 1936 vs. Brooklyn
b) 1972 vs. Oakland
c) 1962 vs. Detroit
d) 1947 vs. Philadelphia

•

14 What future *Pittsburgh Press* sportswriter was a scout for the Steelers in the 1940s?

•

15 What Steelers draft pick was called "the next John Hannah"?

a) Tom Ricketts
b) John Rienstra
c) John Jackson
d) Brian Blankenship

•

16 Who was Chuck Noll talking about when he said, "I'm in love with him"?

a) Rod Woodson
b) Dick Haley
c) Darryl Sims
d) Terry Bradshaw

•

17 What was the first pro football job each of these Steelers executives held: Tom Donahoe, Jim Boston, Dan Rooney, Art Rooney II?

•

18 True or False: Franco Harris, who played 12 seasons with the Steelers, led them in rushing each of those years.

•

19 True or False: Neither of the two games between the Pittsburgh Steelers and Philadelphia Eagles in 1938 was played in Pennsylvania.

•

20 Which Steelers head coach died during his tenure with the team?

•

21 Can you name the 22 players on all four Steelers Super Bowl teams?

•

22 Who called the 1986 Steelers' defense "soft and cheesey"?

a) Bubby Brister
b) Chuck Noll
c) Bob Trumpy
d) Dwight White

•

23 Name three Hall of Fame quarterbacks drafted by the Steelers.

•

24 1985 number one draft pick Darryl Sims listed this as his favorite color.

•

25 What other three nicknames have the Steelers gone by?

•

26 The Steelers won their first Super Bowl in 1974. Who led them in passing that season?

•

27 Who was supposed to be the primary receiver on the "Immaculate Reception" in 1972?

•

28 What Steeler fired shots at a police helicopter?

•

29 What two men coached the Steelers in at least three different decades?

•

30 Name the five Rooney brothers who own the Steelers.

•

31 Which Steeler had the most Pro Bowl appearances?

•

32 How much did Art Rooney pay to start the Pittsburgh franchise in 1933?

•

33 Which Steeler earned his law degree before his playing days ended?

•

34 Chuck Noll was sued after he said which player was part of the NFL's "Criminal Element"?

•

35 Which Steeler held out the entire 1988 season based on a contract dispute?

•

36 When and where was Art Rooney born?

•

37 In what sport did Art Rooney have a chance to make the 1920 Olympics?

•

38 What Steeler led the NFL in rushing and interceptions in 1946?

•

39 On what date were the Steelers founded?

•

40 What did SOS stand for?

•

41 Name the former Steeler who opened homes for wayward youths after his retirement in 1983.

•

42 Name the Ice Capades star who married Terry Bradshaw.

•

43 Name the Steeler from the 1970s who enjoyed riding with Pittsburgh cops on duty.

•

44 "Three Bricks Shy of a Load" was:

a) A song sung by Frank Sinatra and dedicated to the Steelers

b) Buddy Parker talking about Big Daddy Lipscombe

c) A book written by Roy Blount Jr. about the 1973 Steelers

d) Joe Walton describing Bubby Brister

•

45 Which player holds the record for most games played by a Steeler?

•

46 Name the first three Steelers to go to the Pro Bowl.

•

47 The Steelers' first draft pick was named after what famous playwright?

•

48 Who holds the record for most passing yards for the Steelers in one game?

•

49 In 1988, who said, "I'm the man. Write it down"?

a) Mike Merriweather
b) Bubby Brister
c) Chuck Noll
d) Aaron Jones.

•

50 What was the only team to lose to Chuck Noll's first team in 1969?

ANSWERS TO 50 QUESTIONS

1 Jack Lambert.

2 Steve Bono.

3 c) Lambert injured his toe during the 1984 season and was never the same.

4 The Chicago Bears.

5 b) Joe Paterno, who decided to remain at Penn State.

6 False. L. C. Greenwood is the career leader with 73½. Greene is second with 66.

7 Cornerback Mel Blount, after he got beat that day by Oakland's Cliff Branch.

8 Bill Dudley, Hall of Fame back, who played for the Steelers, Lions, and Redskins from 1942 through 1953.

9 Frank Walton (1947) and Joe Walton (1990–91).

10 Three—Bert Bell, Aldo Donelli, and Walt Kiesling.

11 Offensive tackle Tunch Ilkin's mother, who was Miss Turkey in 1950.

12 b) Rod Woodson signed a contract in 1991 that paid him an average of $1.45 million annually.

13 d) The Steelers tied the Eagles at 8-4 atop the Eastern Conference but lost a playoff to them, 21-0.

14 Pat Livingston, who also did some public relations work for the Steelers before he became a sports writer.

15 b) Guard John Rienstra, their first-round draft pick in 1986 and a Steeler through 1990, when he joined Cleveland as a Plan B free agent.

16 a) Cornerback Rod Woodson, after Noll drafted him in the first round in 1987.

17 All were once Steelers ball boys in training camp.

18 True. No one outrushed Franco Harris during his entire career with the Steelers.

19 True. They were played in Buffalo, New York, and Charleston, West Virginia, that year.

20 Jock Sutherland died from a brain tumor in the spring of 1948, while on a scouting trip.

21 Rocky Bleier, Mel Blount, Terry Bradshaw, Larry Brown, Sam Davis, Steve Furness, Joe Greene, L. C. Greenwood, Randy Grossman, Jack Ham, Franco Harris, Jon Kolb, Jack Lambert, Gerry Mullins, Donnie Shell, John Stallworth, Lynn Swann, J. T. Thomas, Loren Toews, Mike Wagner, Mike Webster, Dwight White.

22 d) Former Steel Curtain member Dwight White.

23 Terry Bradshaw (1970), Johnny Unitas (1955), Len Dawson (1957).

24 Sims said his favorite color was "plaid."

25 Pirates (1933–40), Steagles (1943), Card-Pitts (1944).

26 Joe Gilliam, who passed for 1,274 yards.

27 Wide receiver Barry Pearson, but Terry Bradshaw wound up throwing it to Frenchy Fuqua and Franco Harris wound up catching it.

28 Defensive tackle Ernie Holmes, who went on to play in two Super Bowls as part of the original Steel Curtain.

29 Chuck Noll (four, 1969–91) and Walt Kiesling (1938–39, 1941, 1949–54).

30 The five Rooney brothers—Dan, Art Jr., Tim, and twins John and Pat.

31 Joe Greene, 10 Pro Bowls.

32 $2,500.

33 Cornerback Dwayne Woodruff (1979–1990).

34 The Raiders' George Atkinson.

35 Linebacker Mike Merriweather, who was traded after the season to the Minnesota Vikings.

36 Art Rooney was born in 1901 in Coulterville, Pennsylvania.

37 Rooney was named to the U.S. boxing team but did not participate.

38 Bill Dudley, who had 604 yards rushing and 10 interceptions.

39 July 8, 1933.

40 Same Old Steelers, a line once uttered by Art Rooney that stuck through the bad times.

41 There are two Mel Blount Youth Homes, one in Georgia and one in Pennsylvania.

42 Jo Jo Starbuck, Bradshaw's second wife.

43 Hall of Fame linebacker Jack Lambert.

44 c) The book by Roy Blount Jr. was written one year before they won their first Super Bowl.

45 Center Mike Webster, 220 games.

46 Joe Geri, Jerry Shipley, and Bill Walsh (1951).

47 Bill Shakespeare, Notre Dame (1936).

48 Bobby Layne—409 yards on December 14, 1958, against the Chicago Cardinals.

49 b) Bubby Brister, who was competing for the starting quarterback job with Todd Blackledge.

50 Detroit lost to the Steelers, 16-13, at Pitt Stadium.

Joe Greene, displaying the Steelers' logo

THE MYSTERY BEHIND THE LOGO

It's not exactly Stonehenge, but the mystery surrounding the Steelers' logo on their helmet has baffled fans for more than three decades.

The now-familiar logo, adopted from the steel industry, first appeared on helmets in the 1962 season. But they appeared only on the right side. The left side of the helmet remained bare. In 1963, the Steelers switched from gold helmets to black and they have worn black ever since. The logo, however, remained only on the right side.

More than 30 years later, the Steelers still get phone calls and letters asking why the logo appears on only the right side of the helmet, but it has remained cloaked in mystery.

Now, we have the answer to one of the longest-running trivia questions in Pittsburgh Steelers history.

One theory had it that the late Jackie Hart, the irascible Steelers field manager, refused to put the logo on both sides of the helmet because it was twice the work. Not true.

First, some background.

"Republic Steel Company came to us and said, 'You're the Steelers, why not put the steel logo on your helmet?' " Steelers president Dan Rooney related.

That is the first irony—Republic was based in Cleveland, Pittsburgh's hated rival.

United States Steel Corporation actually developed the logo and eventually permitted its use to identify the entire industry.

The Steelers used it experimentally and it was so well received, they adopted it. At first, the logo consisted of a circle enclosing three hypercycloids and the word "Steel." In 1963, the Steelers got permission from the Iron and Steel Institute to change the word in the logo to "Steelers."

The Steelers continued to carry the logo only on the right side of the helmets. Some United Steel Workers even suggested they carry the union label on the other side, but to this day the left side of the helmet is bare.

But why?

"When we first used it, we weren't sure how it would work out," Rooney explained, "so we only put it on one side. Then it became a curiosity thing. Everyone wanted to know why we put it only on one side. So we said let's keep it on one side of the helmet. It's created a lot of interest. Everyone talks about it. We still get phone calls and letters asking us about it."

Now you know the answer.

Hall of Fame
Word Search

Find the Steelers' Hall of Famers. The year tells when the player was inducted into the Hall of Fame.

NAME	*YEAR*
BELL (Bert)	1963
BLOUNT (Mel)	1989
BRADSHAW (Terry)	1989
DUDLEY (Bill)	1966
GREENE (Joe)	1987
HAM (Jack)	1988
HARRIS (Franco)	1990
JOHNSON (John Henry)	1987
KIESLING (Walt)	1966
LAMBERT (Jack)	1990
LAYNE (Bobby)	1967
McNALLY (Johnny)	1963
NOLL (Chuck)	1993
ROONEY (Art)	1964
STAUTNER (Ernie)	1969

R O O N T R S A F J R S Y V E T B S T L N E E J S R

J N E S G E N T V G L R C S I T E H A I N R V L Z X

H O A L N E M C J B L L O O R K L I E S M A L H R A

C A H R G R E E W E B S O W T A L V N H A O F A N S

A T T N E T H R I S T C R N O I M P D A S E R V E H

R E C S S I R O O N E Y O F D U D L S P Y V A T W B

O T H E C O A R C E O T U B W I V D E R S E P L E R

N O S H L E N Y S I N G A M N A P C C N E T J E X A

T E F R K E N W O L O L M I L G R T E M A H D D A D

L N S O N B A M F S I R R A H S E H S H I O S P F S

A F I V L A M B F O U I W N S A T F R I M E U X Z H

Y S X E L V E K N Y E L L A R D E N E A Z E D R E A

N W R E D O G S G L G T V G D O U G S N O G I C E W

E C U B P U B E N M Y O D O R C O W D P O U W E G Q

M Z D T I G I D N L D E G R N D C Y L P H L S L T N

P E U P A T R B L C L L D Q S T L A T E I A I C T N

W A A B U T L A W D O C Y B T T P C G E Y T B U Z Y

N G M C P O N S K S H W R B Z A S G B L K S H E P I

S H N A S C Q P U B A D U Z T H M E I N V S N N S T

Y L E S M H K Q U L O H U R I S O N K L L A H E M E

S K E Z D U Z T N O O T K I E S L I N G C A N E D I

B T A H U N M I S U R U R N B L C M F A L F K R L A

W I L P R E D R H N M P Z E G R M S S M L L O G N T

A H L D U Y B K T T E R X M B K N T R B D E D N D K

S T R F M Y Z I N G Z E X P A M Q T S H A S Y N D R

R Y N E C B R A D S L A D I E L A E S K I P A B L S

C L D S T A U T N E R R Y M N Y E L Y A L K D A L L

John Henry Johnson

Jack Ham and Joe Paterno

Bobby Layne

Johnny "Blood" McNally

Jack Lambert

PAIR THE STEELER WITH HIS ALMA MATER

1 Fran Rogel
2 Bill Walsh
3 Barry Foster
4 Bryan Hinkle
5 Ernie Holmes
6 Andy Russell
7 Mel Blount
8 Dwight White
9 Dave Smith
10 George Tarasovic
11 Silvio Zaninelli
12 Dick Shiner
13 Jim Finks
14 Robin Cole
15 Randy Grossman
16 Tunch Ilkin
17 Roy Jefferson
18 Jack Butler
19 Lynn Chandnois
20 Dick Haley

a) East Texas State
b) Utah
c) Pitt
d) Duquesne
e) Tulsa
f) Penn State
g) St. Bonaventure
h) Arkansas
i) New Mexico
j) Michigan State
k) Missouri
l) Indiana State
m) Texas Southern
n) Oregon
o) Maryland
p) LSU
q) Southern
r) Temple
s) Notre Dame
t) Indiana University of Pennsylvania

ANSWERS: 8-a, 17-b, 20-c, 9-t, 13-e, 1-f, 18-g, 3-h, 14-i, 19-j, 6-k, 16-l, 5-m, 4-n, 12-o, 10-p, 7-q, 15-r, 2-s, 11-d.

HIP, HIP—YES, THE STEELERS HAD CHEERLEADERS

They do it in Dallas, in Philadelphia, in Miami, in Los Angeles, in New England, Houston, Minnesota, and throughout North America.

But they don't do it in Pittsburgh. The Steelers do not have cheerleaders. Never have, never will. Right? Maybe they never will *again,* but they once did.

Throughout the 1970s, 1980s, and now the 1990s the Steelers have steadfastly refused to join the NFL bandwagon and hire cheerleaders or dancers. While the Cowboys had their Dallas Cowboys Cheerleaders, the Rams had their Embraceable Ewes, and the Oilers had their Derrick Dolls, the closest thing the Steelers had to cheerleaders was Franco's Italian Army.

But long before the Cowboys and others introduced their fancy, new-wave cheerleaders, the Steelers actually had official cheerleaders.

They were called the Steelerettes and they would strut their stuff along the sidelines from 1961 through 1969.

"We got the idea before all these 'professional' cheerleaders came into vogue," said Steelers president Dan Rooney.

These girls were a far cry from the dancers in their skintight, itty-bitty costumes that perform as cheerleaders today. These were coeds from Robert Morris College in Pittsburgh, eight of them, hired by the Steelers and selected in tryouts for their ability and All-American values, which included good grades. They dressed in the traditional attire of high school cheerleaders of the times.

"This clearly was a little different than leading cheers," says Bill Day, who handled the Steelers' entertainment in those days as well as serving as a vice president at Robert Morris. "It was more acrobatics and forming pyramids than trying to lead a crowd.

"Back in those days, we were trying to sell tickets any way we could."

The Steelerettes cheered at home games and, for a few years, had male counterparts called the Ingots. Both groups wore hard-hats for awhile and they also used the same type of airhorns miners once had, the better to keep the crowds awake when their heroes on the field could not.

"It was a thing for the times," Day said. "The fans seemed to enjoy it."

The Ingots' days were doomed, however, after an overly enthusiastic display near the end zone in the mid-1960s. The men were in charge of firing off a cannon that carried a powder charge whenever the Steelers scored. One fine Sunday, as wide receiver Buddy Dial raced into the end zone, the Ingots prematurely set off their cannon within several yards of Dial. Witnesses claim Dial never jumped so high.

"That," Day said, "was sort of the end of the Ingots."

The Steelerettes last performed during the 1969 season. The Steelers moved into a new stadium at the confluence of the Three Rivers in 1970 and the quaint, old-fashioned cheerleaders really were out of style. It was time for the Steelers to either opt for the modern version or do without.

"You could see the Cowboy thing coming with less and less clothing on the kids," Day said. "That's really not what Mr. Rooney had in mind. You know how the Rooneys are. They wanted something in good taste. They didn't want all that flesh showing."

The Rooneys also did not think the cheerleaders added much to the excitement of the pro game.

"We have found that our fans do the cheering for us," Dan Rooney said. "They were rated the most knowledgeable fans in the league. We're letting them lead the cheers."

Steeler cheerleaders? Gone and, for the most part, forgotten.

First Quarter

50 QUESTIONS

1 How many times did Franco Harris lead the AFC in rushing?

a) None
b) 5
c) 3
d) 1

•

2 What was the name of the bar near St. Vincent College the Steelers of the early 1970s frequented?

a) Dante's
b) Noll's Hideaway
c) Quarterback Club
d) 19th Hole

•

3 What was Rooney U?

a) A small college in West Virginia named after the Rooney Family
b) A sportswriter's nickname for the Pittsburgh franchise
c) The summer nickname of St. Vincent College
d) A turnaround on the Pennsylvania Turnpike near Monroeville

•

4 Which seven of the following players were drafted by the Steelers?

a) Gary Anderson
b) Rocky Bleier
c) Paul Martha
d) Hugh Lickiss
e) Sam Huff
f) Emerson Boozer
g) Brent Jones
h) Ben McGee
i) Donnie Shell
j) Wonder Monds

•

5 Of the following, who never won the Steelers' MVP Award?

a) Mel Blount
b) Franco Harris
c) Glen Edwards
d) Lynn Swann

Franco Harris

•

6 Match the book about the Steelers with its author:

1 *Lost Sundays*	a) Terry Bradshaw
2 *Three Bricks Shy of a Load*	b) Jim O'Brien
3 *Looking Deep*	c) Rocky Bleier
4 *Dawn of a New Steel Age*	d) Sam Toperoff
5 *Fighting Back*	e) Ed Bouchette
6 *Whatever It Takes*	f) Roy Blount Jr.

•

7 Which of these quarterbacks were the property of the Steelers in the 1950s?

a) Johnny Unitas
b) Jack Kemp
c) Len Dawson
d) Jim Finks
e) Earl Morrall
f) Ted Marchibroda
g) Answers *a* and *d*
h) None
i) All

•

8 Who said Terry Bradshaw couldn't spell "cat" if you spotted him "c-a"?

a) Hollywood Henderson
b) Chuck Noll
c) Burt Reynolds
d) Jack Tatum
e) Jack Lambert

•

9 What was the longest rookie holdout in Steelers history?

•

10 Which Steeler went on to serve on the U.S. Supreme Court?

•

11 Name the Steelers' wide receiver who spiked the ball on the five yard line instead of the end zone and lost a touchdown on "Monday Night Football" in 1971?

•

12 What rookie was killed driving to training camp on Route 30 in 1977?

•

13 True or False: Fabian was once drafted by the Steelers.

•

14 In 1956 the Steelers got the NFL bonus pick in the draft. Name the player and his college.

•

15 What Big Ten basketball coach was a Steelers draft choice?

•

16 In 1959 there were 30 rounds in the draft. How many players did the Steelers draft in the first seven rounds?

•

17 Who scored the final touchdown under Chuck Noll?

•

18 True or False: In the 1970s the Steelers played in Three Rivers Stadium, Pitt Stadium, and Forbes Field.

•

19 Who was the head coach before Chuck Noll?

•

20 The so-called "cheap" Steelers paid the highest NFL rookie salary ever to what draft choice in 1938?

•

21 Name an owner of the Steelers not named Rooney.

a) Baldy Regan
b) Chuck Noll
c) Jack McGinley
d) City of Pittsburgh

•

22 True or False: Bill Cowher's wife, Kaye, played pro basketball.

•

23 Which two Steelers were voted among the top three players at their positions in the NFL's first 50 years, in a Hall of Fame poll?

a) Jack Butler, defensive back
b) Ernie Stautner, defensive tackle
c) Bill Dudley, back
d) Marion Motley, back
e) Lupe Sanchez, defensive back

•

24 When asked how he wanted to be remembered, who said, "Don't leave anything on the beach but your footprints"?

a) Art Rooney Sr.
b) Terry Bradshaw
c) Tim Worley
d) Chuck Noll

•

25 What Steelers first-round draft pick was crippled by an auto accident during his rookie season?

•

26 True or False: Rocky Bleier outgained O. J. Simpson in a 1974 playoff game versus the Buffalo Bills in Three Rivers Stadium.

•

27 What was the name of the division the Steelers played in before they moved to the AFC Central?

•

28 What assistant coach declined an offer in 1983 to become head coach of the USFL Pittsburgh Maulers?

•

29 What is the most common last name of those who have played for the Steelers?

•

30 Which Steeler intercepted a pass and threw an interception in the same game in the 1970s?

•

31 Who invented the Terrible Towel?

a) Lynn Swann
b) Jack Fleming
c) Bob Prince
d) Myron Cope

•

32 What linebacker in the Steelers' 1971 training camp went on to be a head coach in Cleveland and Kansas City?

•

33 What work did the father of Art Rooney Sr. do?

a) Saloon keeper
b) Coal miner
c) Sportswriter
d) City councilman

•

34 Why didn't Pittsburgh have an NFL team before 1933?

•

35 What was the name of Art Rooney's semi-pro team that joined the NFL in 1933?

a) Ironmen
b) Pirates
c) Rooney Tunes
d) North Side Bulldogs
e) Majestic Radios

•

36 Who was the Steelers' first black player?

•

37 Name one of the Steelers' two player-coaches.

•

38 Which Steeler became their first kicking specialist?

•

39 When were the Pittsburgh Pirates first called the Steelers?

•

40 Who was the only Steeler to pass for more than 1,000 yards between 1933 and 1951?

a) Bill Dudley
b) Jim Finks
c) Joe Geri
d) Johnny Clement

•

41 Which popular defensive tackle died during training camp in 1948 after undergoing an appendectomy?

•

42 Fill in the blank of this popular 1950s chant: "Hi diddle diddle, ______ up the middle."

•

43 Name the players who made up the Steel Curtain front four.

•

44 Name the famous coach who, in 1970, said, "Chuck Noll is building one hell of a football team up in Pittsburgh. I look for the Steelers to be the team of the future. Just remember I said that."

•

45 Which linebacker retired before the 1989 season to attend medical school?

•

46 Where did the Steelers' replacement team train for two weeks before the strike games in 1987?

a) Latrobe
b) Pittsburgh
c) Homestead
d) Johnstown
e) David Lawrence Convention Center

•

47 How many number one draft picks did the Steelers have in the 10 years between 1958 and 1967?

•

48 What is Rocky Bleier's real first name?

a) Robert
b) Rocky
c) Frances
d) Ricky

•

49 Which number one draft choice did the Steelers lose in the 1976 NFL expansion draft?

•

50 Who said, "I'm more pumped up than the U.S. Blimp"?

a) Bubby Brister
b) Ernie Holmes
c) Steve Courson
d) John Rienstra

ANSWERS TO 50 QUESTIONS

1 a) Franco Harris, one of the NFL's all-time rushing leaders, never won a rushing title.

2 d.

3 b) It was a named popularized by sportswriter Jack Sell of the *Pittsburgh Post-Gazette.*

4 b) Bleier; c) Martha; d) Lickiss; f) Boozer g) Jones; h) McGee; j) Monds.

5 d.

6 1-d, 2-f, 3-a, 4-e, 5-c, 6-b.

7 i) All were either drafted or signed by them.

8 a) Henderson, before Pittsburgh and Dallas played in Super Bowl XIII.

9 Rod Woodson signed a contract on October 28, 1987, 94 days after training camp opened.

10 Byron "Whizzer" White.

11 Dave Smith vs. Kansas City.

12 Defensive tackle Randy Frisch, seventh-round draft choice from Missouri.

13 True. Fabian Hoffman, an end from Pitt, was drafted on the 13th round in 1939.

14 Gary Glick, Colorado State.

15 Purdue's Gene Keady, 19th round, 1958, from Kansas State.

16 None. They traded all seven picks.

17 Richard Shelton vs. Cleveland on an interception return.

18 False. They began play in Three Rivers Stadium in 1970 and played all their home games there.

19 Bill Austin, 1966–68. His record was 11-28-3.

20 Byron "Whizzer" White, $15,800.

21 c) Jack McGinley, Art Rooney's brother-in-law.

22 True. She played for the New York Stars in the Women's Professional Basketball League.

23 a, b.

24 d.

25 Gabe Rivera, October 1983.

26 True. He gained 99 yards rushing and receiving to 83 for Simpson.

27 Century Division.

28 Dick Hoak, their running backs coach.

29 Williams.

30 Tony Dungy vs. Houston, 1977. A defensive back, Dungy was pressed into service at quarterback when both Terry Bradshaw and Mike Kruczek were injured that day.

31 d.

32 Marty Schottenheimer.

33 a.

34 Pennsylvania's blue laws forbade Sunday play.

35 e.

36 Tackle Ray Kemp, 1933.

37 Forrest Douds or Johnny McNally.

38 Armand Niccolai (1934–42).

39 1941.

40 d) Clement passed for 1,004 yards in 1947.

41 Tackle Ralph Calcagni.

42 Rogel (Fran Rogel, 1950–57).

43 Dwight White, Ernie Holmes/Steve Furness, Joe Greene, L. C. Greenwood.

44 Vince Lombardi.

45 Gregg Carr.

46 d) Johnstown.

47 Four; the rest were traded away.

48 a) Robert.

49 Defensive back Dave Brown, taken in the expansion draft by the Seattle Seahawks.

50 b) Ernie Holmes, excited before a big game.

STEEL CURTAIN CALL

To football fans in Pittsburgh, two questions rank right up there with "Who was the Beatles' drummer before Ringo Starr?" and "What were they called before they were called the Beatles?"

1 Who was the defensive tackle on the Steel Curtain before Ernie Holmes?

2 What was it called before it was called the Steel Curtain?

The familiar Steel Curtain defensive line was formed by ends Dwight White and L. C. Greenwood, and tackles Joe Greene and Ernie Holmes. In 1977, Steve Furness replaced Holmes, who was traded a year later to the Tampa Bay Buccaneers.

But who *preceded* Holmes?

Holmes joined White, Greene, and Greenwood in 1972 as a starter. But in 1971, before Holmes, the other three started in the defensive line together. The fourth spot in that line was filled alternately by two tackles—Lloyd Voss, a player acquired from Vince Lombardi's Green Bay Packers in 1966, and Big Ben McGee, the Steelers' fourth-round draft pick from Jackson State in 1964.

In 1971, however, it was not called the Steel Curtain. In fact, it wasn't called much of anything except the Steelers' front four.

The real Steel Curtain made its debut in 1972, coinciding with Holmes's appearance and resulting in the Steelers' first AFC Central Division championship.

But who named it the Steel Curtain?

The answer lies somewhere in a discussion several people had one day about the magnificent front four of White, Holmes, Greene, and Greenwood. Two of those in the group were Pat Livingston, the *Pittsburgh Press* sports editor and columnist, and Joe Gordon, the Steelers' public relations director.

Someone said the front four deserved a nickname. Livingston liked the idea of using the word "curtain" to describe them. Someone suggested they call it the Black Curtain. A few liked that idea, but others thought some people might become offended because

White, Holmes, Greene, and Greenwood were all black.

"I liked the idea of the curtain," Livingston said, "because they just blanketed everything. It was hard to get through those guys. They separated the field."

Then, someone piped up, "Why not the Steel Curtain?"

Bingo.

Gordon credits Livingston with naming it, although Livingston doesn't remember if he did or not.

"If he didn't name it," Gordon said, "he's the one who popularized it."

The nickname Steel Curtain caught on quickly. Eventually it was used to describe the entire Steelers' defense of the 1970s. But in its original form, the Steel Curtain described one of the most dominant front fours in the history of pro football:

White, Holmes, Greene, Greenwood.

The Steel Curtain: Dwight White, Ernie Holmes, Joe Greene, and L. C. Greenwood

STEELERS' NICKNAMES

Match the Steeler with his nickname.

1 Bill Dudley	a) Red
2 Sidney Thornton	b) Hollywood Bags
3 Joe Gilliam	c) Mad Dog
4 Ed Farrell	d) Jap
5 Byron White	e) Dirt
6 John Fuqua	f) Fats
7 Chuck Noll	g) Whizzer
8 Jim Butler	h) Bullet
9 Gene Lipscomb	i) Thundering Bull
10 Art Rooney	j) Jefferson Street
11 Reggie Harrison	k) Scrapper
12 Forrest Douds	l) The Pope
13 Willis Thompson	m) Frenchy
14 Mel Blount	n) The Chief
15 L. C. Greenwood	o) Moon
16 Dennis Winston	p) Weegie
17 Bill Mack	q) Big Daddy
18 Ernie Holmes	r) Boobie
19 Dwight White	s) Supe
20 Gerry Mullins	t) Cannonball

ANSWERS: 1-h, 2-i, 3-j, 4-k, 5-g, 6-m, 7-l, 8-t, 9-q, 10-n, 11-r, 12-d, 13-p, 14-s, 15-b, 16-e, 17-a, 18-f, 19-c, 20-o.

Coach Buddy Parker and Bobby Layne on the sidelines

15 SHORT SNAPS

1 Season tickets for six Steelers home games in 1952 cost between $15.60 and $31.20 per seat.

•

2 Art Rooney nearly drowned in Pittsburgh's baseball stadium? Rooney often told this story:

When he was a young boy, Exposition Park, the old baseball field situated where Three Rivers Stadium is today, occasionally flooded when the rivers rose. One day, he and his older brother, Dan, and a friend were in a canoe in the outfield at Exposition Park when the canoe tipped. Dan and the friend scrambled out and swam toward the seats. But young Art was wearing a thick pair of rubber boots and struggled. Dan came to his aid to save the day—and the future owner of the Pittsburgh Steelers.

•

3 Pittsburgh abandoned the Single Wing offense in 1952 in favor of the T-formation, the last pro team to do so.

•

4 NFL Commissioner Bert Bell, once a part owner of the Steelers with Art Rooney in the 1940s, died of a heart attack at Franklin Field in Philadelphia during the final two minutes of the Eagles-Steelers game on October 11, 1959. Philadelphia won the game, 28-24.

•

5 The Steelers beat the College All-Stars 24-0 in a 1976 exhibition game shortened because of a severe thunder storm in Chicago. It was the last such game played between the NFL and the college seniors, the series having begun in 1934.

•

6 Art Rooney died on August 25, 1988, following a stroke. He was 87.

•

7 Before the 1957 season, Coach Buddy Parker traded number one draft picks in 1958 and 1959, and linebacker Marv Matuszak to

San Francisco for quarterback Earl Morrall and guard Mike Sandusky. One year later, Parker turned around and traded Morrall and the team's number two pick in 1959 and the number four pick in 1960 for quarterback Bobby Layne.

In essence, he traded the team's number one pick in 1958, its number one and two picks in 1959 and the number four pick in 1960 along with linebacker Marv Matuszak for Layne and Sandusky. He was probably worth it. Layne threw for 8,983 yards in five seasons and the Steelers finished with winning records three times, including a second-place finish in 1962 (9-5).

•

8 The Steelers first appeared on "Monday Night Football" on November 2, 1970, when they beat Cincinnati 21-10 in Three Rivers Stadium.

•

9 Before 1992, Pittsburgh backs had rushed 31 times or more in a game only four times in history. Barry Foster did it three times alone in 1992 (33 twice and 31).

•

10 Another myth exposed! Coach Chuck Noll preached that you build teams with defense. But he did not follow that philosophy in his early drafts with the Steelers. His first four; drafts were dominated by offensive players. In 1969, four of his top five picks were on offense; in 1970, five of the top six; in 1971, three of his first four; and in 1972, his first three picks were offensive players.

•

11 Art Rooney played minor league baseball from 1920 to 1925.

•

12 Within a four-month period in 1978, Chuck Noll made his two worst trades in 23 seasons with the Steelers:

—On April 17, he traded guard Jim Clack and wide receiver Ernie Pough to the New York Giants for guard John Hicks.

—On August 15, he traded wide receiver Frank Lewis to Buffalo for tight end Paul Seymour.

Hicks (cut) and Seymour (failed physical) never played for the Steelers. The Lewis and Clack expedition continued long, productive careers with their new teams.

•

13 Center Mike Webster is the only player of the 22 four-time Super Bowl winners who left the Steelers through free agency and joined another team. Webster also may be the only player in their

Chuck Noll

history to twice "retire" and return to play without ever missing a game.

Webster announced his retirement in a huff after the 1987 season following a dispute with the club over pay for the one game lost to the strike that year. He unretired shortly afterward and played in 1988.

He retired a second time after the 1988 season when the Steelers left him unprotected in Plan B free agency. He then accepted a job as a coach with the Kansas City Chiefs. A few months later, he gave up his coaching job and signed with the Chiefs as a player and started at center for them the next two seasons.

•

14 Cleveland's Marion Motley set an NFL single-game record by averaging 17.09 yards per rush (11 for 188 yards) against the Steelers on October 29, 1950. It is one of the 10 longest-running records in NFL history. Motley, a Hall of Famer, played his entire career with the Browns except for a brief stay with the Steelers in 1955, when he carried two times for eight yards. He then called it quits for good.

•

15 Rex Johnston of Southern Cal was a back with the Steelers in 1960. Four years later, he made it to baseball's major leagues with the Pirates. An outfielder, he played in 14 games with the Bucs and had no hits in seven at bats and never played again in the majors—baseball or football.

CALL HIM HULK HASELRIG

You'll need an NCAA guide, not a football encyclopedia, to look up the answer to this question: Who is the only wrestler to win six NCAA heavyweight championships?

Answer: Steelers offensive guard Carlton Haselrig. While attending the University of Pittsburgh at Johnstown, Haselrig, in three consecutive years, won the heavyweight wrestling championships in both NCAA Divisions I and II.

The NCAA no longer allows a wrestler to compete in both divisions, so Haselrig has a headlock on the history books. Nobody did it before and nobody can ever do it again. Haselrig's record in college was 143-2-1, both losses coming his freshman season.

If that isn't unique enough, Haselrig overcame a large obstacle to become the Steelers' starting right guard. He never played college football because Pitt-Johnstown did not have a team. He was all-state in football at Johnstown High School, then did not play the sport for the next four years as he concentrated on his wrestling career.

Nevertheless, the Steelers recognized something when they drafted him on the 12th round in 1989. It appeared to be almost a throwback to the 1940s, when the Steelers would draft from *Street & Smith's College Football* magazine. Only this time, they seemed to be getting their picks out of a wrestling magazine.

Haselrig spent his first season on the Steelers' developmental squad, first as a nose tackle. Chuck Noll moved him to guard later that year. Haselrig made the team's active roster in 1990 and played in all 16 games as a backup. He became the starting right guard in 1991.

"Things couldn't have worked out better," he said. "Look where I'm at—I'm in the NFL. A lot of guys who played college football aren't in the NFL."

Haselrig took another step when he was voted to the Pro Bowl in 1992, becoming the first Steelers guard to do so in 18 years.

Carlton Haselrig

"When Chuck first moved me from defense to offense, I didn't care where I was going to play," Haselrig said. "I just wanted to make the roster. Chuck gets all the credit for moving me over, but I definitely wouldn't be here today if it wasn't for the developmental squad."

Haselrig, who is 6 feet 1, 290 pounds, believes his wrestling career served him well in his new profession.

"I have to go against one man still," he said, "and I don't want one man to beat me in anything."

Haselrig has already made it into the Hall of Fame—the Pennsylvania Wrestling Coaches' Hall of Fame.

Head Coaches Word Search

Find the Steelers' head coaches.

NAME	*YEARS*
AUSTIN (Bill)	1966–68
BACH (Joe)	1935–36, 1952–53
BELL (Bert)	1941
COWHER (Bill)	1992–
DIMELIO (Luby)	1934
DONELLI (Aldo)	1941
DOUDS (Forrest)	1933
KIESLING (Walt)	1939–40, 1941–44, 1954–56
LEONARD (Jim)	1945
McNALLY (Johnny)	1937–39
MICHELOSEN (John)	1948–51
NIXON (Mike)	1965
NOLL (Chuck)	1969–91
PARKER (Buddy)	1957–64
SUTHERLAND (Jock)	1946–47

X A S L R J M P G N I L S E I K W K R T O N L W N L
J O N N E L T O A M P F R A N T L O C A G O S O T S
U L A V E R E W O R E T S G L A E D A M I N X E L T
S L T R N F N U L L M L N B N H N L B I A I R L C E
T I N N F F A L E G O S E T L T O T N S N A S I T L
N B O D U P E A M P O C N R A I D A M S C K L D O L
L A B I O K E N N Y M O N D O I L E M I D E A L E P
Q C H I A U P I A D I W A N P O L S P I R P I T T O
U H O R F I D A L L E H N Y M O N G A G A I H B O W
R P P B L D I S G H R E K R A P A N D U L I G E I T
S O H I M S O Y F D B R B L E A N P S N I L L L A I
T I M E L X L R E N B A J L D G R T P E N P L L R R
D A I T I L K T A T E K Z J N O I Z F A K J U G W R
F Q U C A D D O R H O Q L L A N R X O G R T R H B L
E T A N E A E N D E M U N J L H E N D R W K E B O A
F G C L R S N S I S A Y F A R E A Y R W A H E D W C
N M G N A N L O Z B E L N D E N T A A R I O S O B F
R E E S U E C A R F L U A J H A R E N D N M Y N N I
O W L U B N Q U E O A T C D T T A N O E B R E E T K
T B K G S S B V N S E R E V U T Y E E V Z A Y L O E
T P C L W H R P H I A O O R S R H A L N Y S U L Y S
S C H L E R L D I M E L M P P Y I F F R E N C I E L
R T M I C H E L O S E N S B R L L U V G R A N A L S

Bill Cowher

SECOND QUARTER

50 QUESTIONS

1 Who caught Terry Bradshaw's last TD pass?

•

2 Who caught Terry Bradshaw's first TD pass?

•

3 Who caught Terry Bradshaw's longest TD pass?

•

4 Which 1970s player wore boots with goldfish swimming in the heels?

•

5 Bill Cowher played for which two NFL teams?

•

6 Where did Bill Cowher play in college?

•

7 True or False: Bill Cowher's parents were Steelers' season ticket holders in the 1950s.

•

8 What was Bill Cowher's nickname as an NFL player?

a) Face
b) Kamikaze
c) Coach
d) Wild Bill

•

9 What was the significance of cornerback Dwayne Woodruff's retirement after the 1990 season?

•

10 Both scouting director Tom Modrak and Tom Donahoe, the director of football operations, graduated from which college?

a) Gonzaga
b) Penn State
c) Notre Dame
d) Indiana University of Pennsylvania.

•

11 Besides Bill Cowher, name the other three finalists to become Steelers head coach in 1992?

•

12 Where did Chuck Noll go to college?

•

13 In 1972 Chuck Noll wanted to draft which player instead of Franco Harris?

•

14 Barry Foster and Joe Greene both came from what town in Texas?

•

15 In which TV pilot for a comedy series did Terry Bradshaw star in 1981?

a) "Hee Haw"
b) "Stockers"
c) "Black Sunday"
d) "Cheers"

•

16 What Cleveland player turned Terry Bradshaw upside down and jammed his head into the ground, injuring his neck in 1976?

•

17 Which of his teams did Art Rooney Sr. think was the best?

•

18 True or False: The "Immaculate Reception" in 1972 brought about the second playoff victory in Steelers history.

•

19 Name the four Steelers who have rushed for 1,000 yards.

•

20 Who was Chuck Noll's first starting quarterback?

•

21 Who was the Steelers' leading rusher in the two seasons before Franco Harris arrived in 1972?

•

22 Army great Doc Blanchard was the Steelers' first-round draft pick in 1946. How many years did he play for them?

•

23 Between 1964 and 1968, how many exhibition games did the Steelers play in Pittsburgh?

•

24 Besides Chuck Noll, which other men coached the Steelers in 100 games?

•

25 The Steelers traded linebacker Mike Merriweather to Minnesota on the day of the 1989 draft for a first-round pick. Who did they draft with it?

•

26 What former Steelers quarterback played baseball for Jim Leyland, now manager of the Pittsburgh Pirates?

•

27 How did the Steelers acquire placekicker Gary Anderson?

a) Signed after a kicking tryout in Blawnox
b) Claimed on waivers from Buffalo
c) Purchased from the South African National Soccer Team
d) Trade with Buffalo

•

28 Where were the Steelers' headquarters before they moved into Three Rivers Stadium?

a) Forbes Field
b) Hilton Hotel
c) Roosevelt Hotel
d) Edison Hotel

•

29 Which Steeler recorded the first safety in Super Bowl history?

•

30 Roy Gerela was the placekicker for the Steelers in their first three Super Bowls. Who kicked for them in their fourth Super Bowl?

•

31 Andy Russell, a rookie in 1963, was not on the team in 1964–65 before resuming play with them in 1966 through 1976. Why?

a) He was hurt
b) He was in Buddy Parker's doghouse and held out
c) He quit to go back to school
d) Military service

•

32 Who said, "I never had a player I didn't like"?

a) Chuck Noll
b) Buddy Parker
c) Art Rooney
d) Gertrude the Groupie

•

33 In 1979, what two Pittsburgh athletes were selected *Sports Illustrated*'s "Sportsmen of the Year"?

•

34 What former great Steeler defensive back heads the NFL's Blesto scouting combine?

•

35 What Hall of Famer threatened to sue Chuck Noll and the Steelers in the 1970s?

•

36 True or False: Before he joined Pittsburgh, Roy Gerela kicked for the Boston Patriots.

•

37 Which member of the Steel Curtain front four went on to additional fame in Miller Lite beer commercials?

•

38 Who started at running back in the 1976 AFC Championship game in Oakland when Franco Harris and Rocky Bleier could not play because of injuries?

•

39 Before he went into coaching, Chuck Noll planned to pursue a career as what?

a) Astronaut
b) Nuclear physicist
c) Agent
d) Teacher

•

40 After Art Rooney died, what did they do with his office at Three Rivers Stadium?

a) Kept it empty the way it was
b) Had his son, Dan Rooney, move into it
c) Converted it into the Art Rooney Library
d) Converted it into the Art Rooney Museum

•

41 Name the Steeler tackle from the 1980s whose wife appeared on the cover of *Sports Illustrated*.

•

42 Name the rookie quarterback who replaced an injured Terry Bradshaw in 1976 and was undefeated in six starts?

•

43 Why did quarterback Cliff Stoudt abruptly leave the Steelers after the 1983 season?

a) He retired from football
b) He jumped to the Birmingham Stallions of the USFL
c) The fans drove him to quit
d) He wanted to get into coaching

•

44 Why did quarterback David Woodley abruptly leave the Steelers after the 1985 season?

a) He retired from football

b) He jumped to the Tampa Bay Bandits of the USFL

c) Chuck Noll cut him

d) He wanted to spend more time with his wife

•

45 Who led the Steelers in 1976 in total yards from scrimmage (rushing and receiving yards combined)?

•

46 Where did the Steelers hold training camp before they moved to St. Vincent College?

•

47 What was the last Steelers game played in Forbes Field?

•

48 Why did Mean Joe Greene win a Clio Award?

a) For most sacks in the NFL

b) As the best defensive lineman in the league

c) For best nickname in sports

d) For a Coca-Cola commercial

•

49 Why did Johnny Clement wear the number 00?

a) It was the year he was born

b) His hero was Jim Otto

c) His nickname was "Zero"

d) He lost a bet

•

50 Who did the Steelers play in Forbes Field on November 24, 1963, two days after John F. Kennedy was assassinated?

ANSWERS TO 50 QUESTIONS

1 Calvin Sweeney vs. the New York Jets, 1983.

2 Ron Shanklin, 1970.

3 Mark Malone, 91 yards on November 8, 1981, in Seattle.

4 Frenchy Fuqua.

5 Cleveland Browns (1980–82) and Philadelphia Eagles (1983–84) as a linebacker and special-teams player.

6 North Carolina State, 1975–78.

7 True.

8 a.

9 He was the last active player from one of their four Super Bowl teams (XIV).

10 d.

11 Dave Wannstedt, Joe Greene, Kevin Gilbride.

12 University of Dayton.

13 Running back Robert Newhouse, who went on to play for Dallas.

14 Duncanville.

15 b) "Stockers," co-starring Mel Tillis.

16 Turkey Joe Jones.

17 The 1976 team (10-4) that lost to Oakland in the AFC Championship game.

18 False. It was their first playoff victory.

19 John Henry Johnson, Franco Harris, Rocky Bleier, and Barry Foster.

20 Dick Shiner, who led the Steelers in passing in 1969 with 1,422 yards.

21 Frenchy Fuqua, 691 yards in 1970, 625 in 1971.

22 None.

23 None.

24 Only Buddy Parker, whose record with them was 51-48-6 from 1957 to 1964.

25 Tom Ricketts, offensive tackle, Pitt.

26 Bubby Brister, in the Florida Instructional League.

27 b.

28 c.

29 Dwight White, 1974 vs. the Vikings.

30 Matt Bahr, who kicked in 1979 and 1980 for Pittsburgh.

31 d.

32 c.

33 Terry Bradshaw of the Steelers and Willie Stargell of the Pirates.

34 Jack Butler (1951–59).

35 Cornerback Mel Blount, after Noll said he was part of the NFL's "criminal element."

36 False. He kicked two years for the Houston Oilers before he joined the Steelers as a free agent.

37 L. C. Greenwood.

38 Reggie Harrison.

39 d) Teacher.

40 c.

41 Tunch Ilkin's wife, Sharon, was a cheerleader at Indiana State and was pictured on the cover of *SI* in 1979 standing next to Indiana State basketball player Larry Bird.

42 Mike Kruczek.

43 b.

44 a, but d is also acceptable.

45 Rocky Bleier, 1,330 yards (1,036 rushing, 294 receiving).

46 The University of Rhode Island in Kingston.

47 The Cincinnati Bengals beat the Steelers, 23-13, in an exhibition game in 1969, the last pro football game played in Forbes Field.

48 d.

49 c.

50 They tied the eventual NFL champion Chicago Bears, 17-17.

THE BEST STEELERS TEAM OF ALL TIME?

On the occasion of the 50th anniversary of the Pittsburgh NFL franchise, fans voted for the all-time Steelers football team.

Not surprisingly, the fans in 1982 chose many of the players who formed the four-time Super Bowl champions of the 1970s. In fact it is difficult to find someone on the team who DID NOT play in the 1970s. Surely, they had some pretty good ballplayers in Pittsburgh before 1972, when they began their string of eight straight years in the playoffs.

Herewith, the Steelers' 50th anniversary team as chosen by the fans, along with some arguments for those who were bypassed and also for those who have played since then who should make it. Perhaps they will pick a new team on the Steelers' 75th anniversary in 2007.

Offense

Wide receivers—John Stallworth and Lynn Swann. No arguments, although if Buddy Dial had played longer than five years with the Steelers, he might have made it. Dial averaged 20.6 yards per catch, the highest in Steelers history and nearly 4½ yards more than either Stallworth (16.2) or Swan (16.3).

Tackles—Larry Brown and Jon Kolb. A finer duo you may never find on one team. They plowed their way through four Super Bowls, clearing yardage for Franco Harris year after year. Frank Varrichione (1955–60) made the Pro Bowl five times in six seasons with the Steelers but he wasn't in their class.

Guards—Sam Davis and Moon Mullins. Again the fans opted for the two starters from the Super Bowl teams, putting the entire Steelers offensive line from those years on the all-time team. John Nisby

(1957–61) was another fine guard and some might argue for him over Mullins.

Center—Mike Webster. Hands down. Not only was he the best center in Steelers history, he was one of the best in NFL history. However, there are those who think Dermontti Dawson has more tools and may someday surpass Webster in all areas of the position.

Tight end—Elbie Nickel. He became the Steelers' first tight end when that position really came into being in the 1950s, after he started out as a split end. Nickel made Pro Bowls as an end, not as a tight end or a split end. John Hilton was a good tight end in the 1960s. Eric Green set most of the Steelers' records for tight ends and excelled at both blocking and receiving. But his Steelers career is not long enough to list him as the best in their history.

Quarterback—Terry Bradshaw. Who can argue this selection? He's not the only Hall of Famer who ever played quarterback for them (see trivia question elsewhere in this book), but he is the only one to play his entire career with Pittsburgh and the only one to win not one but four Super Bowls. He also holds virtually every significant career passing record. Bobby Layne might have given him a run for his money had he played longer with the Steelers.

Running backs—Franco Harris and Rocky Bleier. There are no doubts about either of them—Franco's the best and Rocky doesn't belong here. Harris rushed for 11,950 yards in his 12-year career with the Steelers. No one else has rushed for more than 5,000. Bleier? He was a great guy, a great story, a wounded war veteran who contributed to four Super Bowl champions, a nice complement to Franco. Bleier may have gotten more out of his talent than anyone on those Super Bowl teams. But he rushed for only 3,865 yards in a 12-year career. You can pick any number of Steeler backs who deserve this honor over Bleier. How could anyone pick Bleier over John Henry Johnson, who's in the Hall of Fame? Even Dick Hoak and Frankie Pollard could be chosen over Bleier. His career is still young, but it looks as though Barry Foster should move ahead of all of them to join Franco on the list.

Terry Bradshaw

Defense

Ends—L. C. Greenwood and Dwight White. L. C. Greenwood should be in the Hall of Fame. Bill McPeak (1949–57) was a pretty good end in his time and you might find an argument with some of his peers about putting him here over Dwight White.

Tackles—Joe Greene and Ernie Stautner. Two Hall of Famers from different eras and two of the most famous Steelers of all time. Ernie Holmes was one hell of a defensive tackle for a period of about five years but he's a distant number three.

Linebackers—Jack Ham, Jack Lambert, and Andy Russell. Ham and Lambert are in the Hall of Fame. Many people believe Russell belongs there. He labored many years on the poor teams of the 1960s before he played long enough to earn two Super Bowl rings. If Greg Lloyd continues to play at his current level, he might some day make a good argument. But not now.

Secondaries—Mel Blount, Jack Butler, Donnie Shell, and Mike Wagner. The all-time team of the first 50 years did not differentiate between cornerbacks and safeties. However, Blount was the only true corner; Shell and Wagner were safeties. Butler played both cornerback and safety. Just one question: Who do you bump out of here to insert cornerback Rod Woodson? It has to be done, you know. Even Blount has said Woodson is better than he was, but how do you bump a Hall of Famer? All Butler did was intercept 52 passes in nine seasons, five years fewer than what Blount needed to set the Steelers' record at 57. Butler was one of the best defensive backs in the 1950s and many believe it an injustice that he's not in the Hall of Fame. Let's settle this argument by picking two cornerbacks, Blount and Woodson, and putting Butler at safety with Shell, bumping Wagner off the team.

Special Teams

Placekicker—Roy Gerela. He wouldn't get a vote if it were held today. Gary Anderson, who joined the Steelers just about when the fans began balloting for the 50th anniversary team, has outkicked Gerela in virtually every category by substantial amounts—total

Rod Woodson

points, total field goals, and accuracy. Anderson rates among the top 10 in NFL history in accuracy. No contest.

Punter—Pat Brady. He played only three seasons for the Steelers (1952–54) but averaged 44.5 yards a punt during his career and 46.9 yards in one season alone (1953). Bobby Joe Green (1960–61) does hold the career record at 45.7. Bobby Walden should get some credit for longevity (1968–77) and kicking for two Super Bowl winners, even though his 41.1 yard career average ranks below Harry Newsome's. For lack of a decisive argument, we'll stick with the fans' vote.

Coach—Chuck Noll. No one even close.

THE NUMBERS GAME

Here are 35 significant numbers in Steelers lore:

1 . . . victory for Chuck Noll's first team in 1969.

2 . . . TDs scored by Cleveland's Eric Metcalf on punt returns vs. the Steelers, October 24, 1993.

3 . . . times Terry Bradshaw threw for more than 300 yards in 1979.

4 . . . times Terry Bradshaw threw for more than 300 yards in his career (regular season).

5 . . . whenever they get "One for the Thumb."

6 . . . seasons it took to win four Super Bowls.

7 . . . exhibition games played by the Steelers in 1976 (they went 5-2).

8 . . . seasons in which Franco Harris rushed for more than 1,000 yards.

9 . . . Pro Bowl visits by center Mike Webster.

10 . . . fumbles by the Steagles on October 9, 1943, vs. the New York Giants.

11 . . . the round in which fullback Frank Pollard was drafted (1980).

12 . . . players on a side when the Steelers played the Canadian Football League (CFL) Toronto Argonauts on August 3, 1960.

13 . . . the number worn by the quarterback the Steelers have long regretted not drafting in 1983 (Dan Marino).

14 . . . victories in the regular season, 1978.

15 . . . consecutive passes Bubby Brister completed to set the team record vs. Detroit on October 1, 1989.

16 . . . fumbles recovered by Joe Greene in his career.

17 . . . yards rushing by the Vikings in Super Bowl IX.

18 . . . holes, Chuck Noll's second-favorite game.

19 . . . 01, the year Art Rooney was born.

20 . . . points scored by Bill Dudley to lead the 1945 Steelers.

21 . . . yards, Franco Harris's longest run from scrimmage in 1982.

22 . . . Steeler players who earned four Super Bowl rings.

23 . . . seasons Chuck Noll coached in Pittsburgh.

24 . . . years old, Barry Foster's age when he rushed for 1,690 yards in 1992.

25 . . . the anniversary year celebrated in 1994 by Myron Cope on the Steelers' broadcast team.

26 . . . interceptions Jim Finks threw in 1955.

27 . . . the round in which the Steelers drafted Abe Gibron in 1948.

28 . . . TD passes thrown by Terry Bradshaw in 1978.

29 . . . the number worn by Barry Foster.

30 . . . draft choices in 1951.

31 . . . points scored by the Steelers in their fourth Super Bowl victory, 1980.

32 . . . draft choices traded away by Buddy Parker from 1959–1963.

33 . . . the mystery number on the beer (Rolling Rock) brewed near the Steelers' training camp in Latrobe, Pennsylvania.

34 . . . years old, Bill Cowher's age when he was named coach.

35 . . . first downs gained by Cleveland vs. the Steelers, November 23, 1986.

BIRTHPLACE MATCH GAME

Match the Steeler with his place of birth.

1 Tunch Ilkin	a) Frankfurt, Germany
2 Gary Anderson	b) Canada
3 John Jackson	c) Samoa
4 Franco Harris	d) Turkey
5 Elnardo Webster	e) South Africa
6 Joel Steed	f) Italy
7 Ernie Stautner	g) New Jersey
8 Lonnie Palelei	h) Bavaria, Germany
9 Roy Gerela	i) Okinawa

ANSWERS: 1-d, 2-e, 3-i, 4-g, 5-f, 6-a, 7-h, 8-c, 9-b

CROSSWORD PUZZLE
Top Two Draft Picks of the 1970s

ACROSS

1 1975 1st pick
3 1972 1st pick
6 1977 2nd pick
7 1971 2nd pick
8 1978 2nd pick
10 1971 1st pick
12 1974 1st pick
13 1974 2nd pick
16 1973 1st pick
17 1970 2nd pick
18 1972 2nd pick

DOWN

1 1975 2nd pick
2 1970 1st pick
3 1979 1st pick
4 1976 1st pick
5 1977 1st pick
9 1976 2nd pick
11 1979 2nd pick
14 1978 1st pick
15 1973 2nd pick

Crossword Answers

B	A	R	B	E	R		H	A	R	R	I	S		C
R			R				A							U
O			A				W		C					N
W			D				T	H	O	R	N	T	O	N
N			S				H		L					I
			H	A	M		O		E					N
			A			F	R	Y			P			G
	L	E	W	I	S		N				I			H
							E				N			A
V								S	W	A	N	N		M
A											E			
L	A	M	B	E	R	T					Y			J
E									P					O
N									H					H
T	H	O	M	A	S		S	H	A	N	K	L	I	N
I									R					S
N					G	R	A	V	E	L	L	E		O
E									S					N

THIRD QUARTER

50 QUESTIONS

1 Which future Steeler qualified for the 1984 Olympic Trials in the 100-meter high hurdles?

•

2 Who holds the Steelers' record for most extra points in a game?

a) Gary Anderson
b) Roy Girela
c) Matt Bahr
d) Gary Kerkorian

•

3 The Steelers have sold out every game but one since 1972. Why did that one not sell out?

•

4 What Steeler did Joe Namath say was "the next Jack Ham" during a "Monday Night Football" telecast in 1985?

•

5 When did Jack Fleming join the Steelers' broadcast team?

a) 1958
b) 1933
c) 1971
d) 1949

•

6 When did Myron Cope join the Steelers' broadcast team?

a) 1958
b) 1970
c) 1965
d) 1974

•

7 Who is the Steelers' all-time leading scorer?

•

8 In 1943, Philadelphia and Pittsburgh combined teams. What was the franchise officially called that season?

•

9 Who was the only Steeler to play in all 15 games during the 1987 strike year?

•

10 Name the sportswriter who covered the Steelers for the *Pittsburgh Post-Gazette* from 1933 until his retirement in 1973?

•

11 True or False: Chuck Noll never had a weekly television show.

•

12 How many more TD passes than interceptions did Terry Bradshaw throw in his career?

a) 76
b) 103
c) 31
d) 2

•

13 In 1983, what odd treatment did Terry Bradshaw try on his ailing right elbow?

a) He rubbed Louisiana hot sauce on it
b) He bathed it in pickle juice
c) A healing mynah bird perched on it
d) He dipped it in the healing waters of the Monongahela

•

14 Why did the Steelers buy briefcases for the Houston Oilers when Pittsburgh made the playoffs in 1977?

•

15 Who is the Steelers' rookie of the year award named after?

a) Whizzer White
b) Terry Bradshaw
c) Huey Richardson
d) Joe Greene

•

16 What is the significance of Pittsburgh's 35-35 tie at Denver on September 22, 1974?

•

17 Who was the first Steeler to win the NFL's Most Valuable Player award?

•

18 What is Pittsburgh's record for most points in a game?

•

19 Which numbers have been retired by the Steelers?

•

20 What was Pittsburgh's longest losing streak under Coach Chuck Noll?

•

21 True or False: Before they lost to Kansas City in January 1994, the Steelers never played in overtime in the playoffs.

•

22 The Steelers have had the number one choice three times in the NFL draft. Name the players they picked.

•

23 Who was the only Steeler to lead the NFL in touchdowns scored in one season?

•

24 Which Steeler led the NFL in scoring?

•

25 Who was the first Pittsburgh quarterback to lead the NFL in TD passes?

•

26 Who was the last Steeler to lead the NFL in rushing?

•

27 Which Steeler never led the NFL in pass receiving yards?

a) John Stallworth
b) Lynn Swann
c) Paul Moss
d) Roy Jefferson

•

28 Name the player who succeeded Jack Lambert at inside linebacker when he retired.

•

29 What Steeler defensive starter was forced to miss the 1978 season because of a life-threatening illness?

•

30 Who has the longest run from scrimmage in Pittsburgh history?

a) Franco Harris
b) Walter Abercrombie
c) Dick Hoak
d) Bobby Gage

•

31 Who played the most seasons in a Pittsburgh uniform?

•

32 Who played in the most playoff games for the Steelers?

a) Mel Blount
b) Joe Greene
c) Mike Webster
d) Larry Brown

•

33 Which of these players caught the most passes in a single game?

a) J. R. Wilburn
b) Elbie Nickel
c) Roy Jefferson
d) John Stallworth
e) Charles Lockett

•

34 Who kicked the longest punt in Steelers history?

•

35 What was the Steelers' longest winning streak?

•

36 What were the most points the Steelers and an opponent scored in one game?

•

37 True or False: Al Davis and Chuck Noll were once on the same coaching staff.

•

38 Joe Greene was Chuck Noll's first draft pick in 1969. Who was his second?

•

39 True or False: Chuck Noll was never named Coach of the Year.

•

40 Wide receiver Louis Lipps scored 46 touchdowns in his career. How many rushing TDs did he have?

a) 0
b) 25
c) 4
d) 13
e) 1

•

41 Who was Ray Mathews?

a) He led the Steelers in rushing in the 1950s
b) He led them in scoring in the 1950s
c) He led them in receiving in the 1950s
d) all of the above

•

42 Who is Ray Downey?

a) He played his familiar trumpet during breaks in Steeler games in the 1960s
b) The official scorer at games in Three Rivers Stadium
c) Former Steeler known as Wrong Way Ray for running in the opposite direction with the ball
d) Longtime stadium P.A. announcer for the Steelers

•

43 Who recovered the most fumbles in Steelers history?

a) Joe Greene
b) Jack Butler
c) Harvey Clayton
d) Jack Ham
e) Steve Furness

•

44 Name the player with the most interceptions in Steelers history.

•

45 True or False: Woodson had an interception with the Steelers during Chuck Noll's first year as a coach and in his last.

•

46 Who led the Steelers in sacks during their first Super Bowl season, 1974?

•

47 Who led the Steelers in sacks during their second Super Bowl season, 1975?

•

48 Besides Mike Webster, what other veteran Steeler crossed the picket line during the 1987 strike and played in all three replacement games for them?

•

49 Name the Miami punter whose 37-yard run on a fake led to Miami's first TD in a 21-17 victory over the Steelers in the 1972 AFC Championship game.

•

50 Who caught Terry Bradshaw's first Super Bowl pass and would later make the Pro Bowl as an offensive tackle?

ANSWERS TO 50 QUESTIONS

1 Rod Woodson.

2 d) Gary Kerkorian had 8 extra points vs. the New York Giants in 1952.

3 On October 18, 1987, Pittsburgh beat Indianapolis 21-7 before 34,627 at Three Rivers Stadium, a game that featured replacement players during the NFL strike. Thousands of fans accepted the Steelers' offer of ticket refunds before the game.

4 Linebacker Bryan Hinkle.

5 a.

6 b.

7 Placekicker Gary Anderson.

8 Phil-Pitt Eagles-Steelers, nicknamed the Steagles.

9 Center Mike Webster.

10 Jack Sell.

11 False. He did one with Sam Nover on old WIIC-TV in 1972.

12 d) 212 TDS, 210 interceptions.

13 c.

14 The Steelers made the playoffs because Houston beat Cincinnati on the final day of the season.

15 d) Officially, it's called "The Joe Greene Great Performance Award."

16 It was the first overtime game in regular-season NFL history.

17 Bill Dudley in 1946, when he led the league in rushing, interceptions, and punt returns.

18 Pittsburgh 62, New York Giants 7 on November 30, 1952.

19 None. They are one of only four NFL teams that has not retired a number.

20 16 games. They lost the final 13 games of 1969 and the first three of 1970.

21 False. They defeated Houston 26-23 on Gary Anderson's 50-yard field goal in overtime on December 31, 1989.

22 Bill Dudley in 1942, Gary Glick in 1956, and Terry Bradshaw in 1970.

23 Franco Harris, 14 in 1976 (tied Chuck Foreman of Minnesota).

24 None ever has.

25 Jim Finks, 20 in 1952 (tying Otto Graham).

26 Bill Dudley, 604 yards in 1946.

27 b.

28 David Little.

29 Defensive back J. T. Thomas, who had Boeck's Sarcoidosis, a viral illness. Thomas returned to play from 1979 through 1981.

30 d) Bobby Gage, 97-yard TD run vs. Chicago Bears on December 4, 1949.

31 Mike Webster, 15 seasons (1974–88).

32 d) Larry Brown, 20 games during his 14-year career (1971–74).

33 a) Wilburn, 12 receptions on December 22, 1967, vs. Dallas.

34 Joe Geri, 82 yards on November 20, 1949, vs. Green Bay.

35 12 games, 1978 (8) to 1979 (4).

36 98 on December 8, 1985, in San Diego: Chargers 54, Pittsburgh 44.

37 True. Both were with the Los Angeles/San Diego Chargers of the old American Football League, 1960–62.

38 Terry Hanratty, quarterback, Notre Dame.

39 False. Noll was named AFC Coach of the Year in 1972 by UPI and in 1989 by the Pro Football Writers.

40 c.

41 b.

42 d.

43 d) Ham, 21.

44 Mel Blount, 57 interceptions.

45 True. Marv Woodson had one in 1969 and Rod Woodson had three in 1991.

46 Ernie Holmes, 11½ sacks.

47 Ernie Holmes, 8½ sacks.

48 Running back Earnest Jackson.

49 Larry Seiple.

50 Larry Brown, who began his career as a tight end.

STEELERS VS. RAIDERS, THE ULTIMATE SERIES

Raiders tight end Bob Moore stood on the sidelines in Three Rivers Stadium, his head bandaged white. Moore had gone up against Pittsburgh's finest in 1972 and come out much worse for the wear.

And this was *before* the football game even began. Moore ran headlong into a dispute with Pittsburgh cops the night before that epic December playoff game, and they clubbed him into submission in a case of mistaken identity.

But there was no mistaking the 1970s rivalry between the Pittsburgh Steelers and the then-Oakland Raiders. The picture of Bob Moore all bandaged up on the sidelines was testimony to just how brutal it could get.

"That was the beginning of the Steelers-Raiders rivalry," Moore said. "It set the tempo."

The white-hot series between the Steelers and Raiders has gone down in history as the only time two teams have met for five straight years in the playoffs, from 1972 through 1976. Some also say that, for a brief period, it was the fiercest and most exciting rivalry pro football has ever seen.

"It's the best one I know of," said former Raiders coach John Madden. "I'd take a combination of those two teams and I'd play anyone, anytime."

The teams met in the playoffs in 1972 (which became the famous "Immaculate Reception" game), and 1973, and in the AFC Championship in 1974, 1975, and 1976. The Steelers won in 1972, and the Raiders in 1973. The winners then proceeded to claim the Super Bowls in each of the next three seasons: the Steelers in 1974 and 1975, and the Raiders in 1976.

"The wins over the Raiders were more gratifying for me than the Super Bowls," said Hall of Fame Steelers linebacker Jack Ham. "In those days, I think we were the number one and number two teams in the league."

The series was a love-hate affair between the Rooney family's tradition-steeped Steelers and Al Davis's maverick Raiders. The teams also played four times during the regular season in that five-year stretch to help warm up for their post-season bash.

"A lot of times it wasn't who won the battle on the scoreboard, but who broke up the other team the most," said former Steeler running back John "Frenchy" Fuqua. "That was a game where there was no friendship whatsoever."

"God," said former Raiders linebacker Phil Villapiano, "it was just ugly."

It was that way on and off the field. Villapiano saw his roommate, Moore, beaten up by Pittsburgh cops, and his brother roughed up by Pittsburgh fans.

"My brother got beat up in the stands in Pittsburgh during one game," Villapiano said. "In Pittsburgh, they would boo us so loud I would get chills. I never had that happen in my life. It would exhilarate me; I couldn't wait to get out there and get into it. It was beautiful."

The most famous game of the series produced one of the most famous plays in NFL history—the "Immaculate Reception." It occurred on December 23, 1972, the day after Moore was clubbed, in a first-round playoff game at Three Rivers Stadium.

With only seconds left in the game, the Steelers trailed by a point and had a fourth-and-10 on their 40. Quarterback Terry Bradshaw scrambled away from a heavy rush, and threw a hard desperation pass 20 yards downfield for Fuqua.

Safety Jack Tatum slammed into Fuqua just as the pass arrived. The ball rebounded from that collision back toward the line of scrimmage. Franco Harris, the Steelers' rookie running sensation, was trailing the play and picked the ball out of the air near his shoetops.

Harris raced down the sideline toward the end zone. Those who kept their heads about them on the Steelers' sideline screamed for him to run out of bounds. If he had, the Steelers could then have kicked a field goal to win it; but if Harris had been tackled, the Steelers, who were out of time-outs, would have lost as the clock ran out.

Fortunately for them and for the game's romance, Harris made it 60 yards into the end zone for the winning touchdown with five seconds left. With the extra point, it was Pittsburgh 13, Oakland 7.

The Raiders screamed that Fuqua, not Tatum, had touched the ball that ricocheted to Harris. Back then, the rules did not permit a pass to touch one teammate before another caught it. If the officials ruled it had, the pass would have been incomplete.

"If it had been in Oakland," Tatum said, "it would have been a different call."

Over the next five years, the rivalry remained bitter and highly entertaining. The Steelers accused the Raiders of greasing their jerseys, of taking air out of their football, and of writing obscenities on the ball in Oakland. The Raiders accused the Steelers of watering the sidelines so it would freeze and prevent their receivers from running their sideline routes.

The latter was Pittsburgh's version of the Ice Game, the 1975 AFC Championship game at Three Rivers Stadium. It was frigid in Pittsburgh, 15 degrees. When the two teams took the field Sunday they discovered ice along the sidelines. The Steelers claimed the tarp ripped accidentally overnight and the sidelines froze. The Raiders believe it was done on purpose.

"On Saturday, there's a tarp there and I see everything is good," Madden said. "On Sunday, I couldn't believe it. Here the field is frozen and they've got a hose out there and they're watering it down. I'm standing there watching them, and they're telling me they're trying to melt the ice! I said, 'Hey, it's so cold here it's going to MAKE MORE ICE!' "

It did, too, and the Raiders slipped to a 16-10 loss and the Steelers went on to win their second Super Bowl.

The year before, 1974, the Steelers had beaten the Raiders in Oakland, 33-14, in the AFC Championship game before they won their first Super Bowl.

In 1976 it was payback time for the Raiders. Art Rooney Sr. thought the 1976 Steelers team was his best. It produced two 1,000-yard rushers in Harris and Rocky Bleier, and the Steel Curtain defense may never have been in better form. But Harris and Bleier were injured during Pittsburgh's 40-14 playoff rout of Baltimore the previous week. They did not play in Oakland in the title game and the Raiders walked away with a 24-7 victory to put them in the Super Bowl, which they won.

"I still say to this day," Harris said not long ago, "if we would have been healthy, we would have had three Super Bowls in a row. I felt no one was going to beat us. We were on a roll. The only thing I feel bad about in my whole career is not being able to play in the 1976 championship game. I mean, maybe we could've won six in a row. You never know."

To this day, no team has won three straight Super Bowls.

The Raiders, though, proved their point when they came to Pittsburgh for the second game of the 1977 season and whipped the Steelers (with Harris and Bleier), 16-7. That game ended the bitter rivalry. The teams did not meet for another three years and by then the series had lost its significance.

But for those five seasons, pro football has not seen a better rivalry. Al Davis told Art Rooney that if it weren't for the Steelers, his Raiders would have been considered the best team of all time.

"That was one of the greatest rivalries ever," Tatum said.

Mean Joe Greene loved it.

"That's what made me feel so fortunate, to have played at that time with the Steelers," Greene said. "The high of all highs is to beat a good football team."

Steelers vs. Raiders (1972–1977)

(Home team in caps)

1972 Season	STEELERS 34,	Raiders 28 (Regular season)
	STEELERS 13,	Raiders 7 (Playoff game)
1973 Season	Steelers 17,	RAIDERS 9 (Regular season)
	RAIDERS 33,	Steelers 14 (Playoff game)
1974 Season	Raiders 17,	STEELERS 0 (Regular season)
	Steelers 24,	RAIDERS 13 (AFC Championship)
1975 Season	STEELERS 16,	Raiders 10 (AFC Championship)
1976 Season	RAIDERS 31,	Steelers 28 (Regular season)
	RAIDERS 24,	Steelers 7 (AFC Championship)
1977 Season	Raiders 16,	STEELERS 7 (Regular season)

15 MORE SHORT SNAPS

1 The son of longtime Steelers scout Bill Nunn is also named Bill Nunn, and is an actor. The younger Nunn, a Steeler ball boy in the 1970s, has appeared in several movies directed by Spike Lee and earned acclaim for his work with Harrison Ford in *Regarding Henry* and with Whoopi Goldberg in *Sister Act,* among other parts he has played. Bill Nunn played a cop, not a nun, in *Sister Act.*

•

2 The Steelers played their games in Forbes Field from 1933 through 1957. They began playing in Pitt Stadium in 1958 and split home games between Pitt and Forbes through 1963. Fans, in fact, could buy season ticket plans just for games at Pitt or just for those at Forbes Field each year. They played all their regular season games at Pitt Stadium from 1964 through 1969. Three Rivers Stadium became their home in 1970.

•

3 On August 3, 1960, the Steelers played an exhibition game in Toronto against the Canadian Football League's Argonauts—using CFL rules such as 12 players on a side, three downs, and the bigger field. Bobby Layne threw TD passes of 61 and 40 yards to Buddy Dial and another of 59 yards to Preston Carpenter, as the Steelers swamped their Canadian hosts, 43-16. Cookie Gilchrist scored on a one-yard TD run for Toronto.

•

4 Art Rooney sold the Steelers to Alexis Thompson on December 9, 1940, for $165,000. Rooney then bought a half-interest in the Philadelphia Eagles; Bert Bell owned the other half. On April 5, 1941, Rooney and Bell traded the Eagles to Thompson for the Steelers. When Bell was named NFL Commissioner in 1946, he sold his shares in the Steelers to Rooney and the McGinleys.

•

5 The Steelers got competition in pro football from the Pittsburgh Maulers of the USFL, who existed for one season, 1984. It

wasn't the first time there were two pro football teams in Pittsburgh, however. In 1936 the Pittsburgh Americans competed in the American Football League, the second of four leagues that would go by that name. The Americans finished fourth in the six-team league with a 3-2-1 record in 1936. In 1937 the Americans were 0-3 when they folded.

•

6 Art Rooney Sr. was also a fight promoter. His biggest bout was the 1951 heavyweight championship match won by Jersey Joe Walcott over Ezzard Charles in Pittsburgh.

•

7 In 1938 the Steelers acquired journeyman end Edgar ("Eggs") Manske in a trade with the Chicago Bears for their first-round draft pick in 1939. The Bears used that pick, the second overall, to draft quarterback Sid Luckman from Columbia University. Luckman directed the Bears' new T-formation that won four NFL titles. Acclaimed as one of the greatest quarterbacks in NFL history, Luckman was inducted into the Hall of Fame in 1965. Eggs Manske scrambled out of Pittsburgh after one season.

•

8 The 1974 Steelers' draft was one of the best in NFL history, producing Lynn Swann (first round), Jack Lambert (second), John Stallworth (fourth), and Mike Webster (fifth). They also drafted running back Tommy Reamon from Missouri on the ninth round. Reamon spurned the Steelers and signed with Florida of the fledgling World Football League. Reamon rushed for 1,576 yards and was named the WFL's co-MVP in 1974. When the WFL folded, Reamon came to training camp with the Steelers but did not make the team. He played for the Kansas City Chiefs in 1976, his only season in the NFL.

•

9 In 1933 the Pittsburgh Pirates did not get a first down but still beat the Boston Redskins, 16-14.

•

10 Before arriving at St. Vincent College in Latrobe, Pennsylvania, the Steelers' training camp was bounced around sites like an unwanted orphan. Among those who entertained the Steelers' training camp: the University of Rhode Island, Hershey (Pennsylvania), St. Francis College (Pennsylvania), California State College (Pennsylvania), St. Bonaventure (New York), West Liberty College

(West Virginia), Alliance College (Pennsylvania), and Slippery Rock (Pennsylvania).

•

11 Three different Steelers won the NFL Defensive Player of the Year Award three consecutive seasons—tackle Joe Greene in 1974, cornerback Mel Blount in 1975, and linebacker Jack Lambert in 1976. Pittsburgh waited until 1993 for another when Rod Woodson earned the honor, which is selected by the Associated Press.

•

12 Before a 1984 playoff game, a Denver sportswriter wrote that Steelers running back Frank Pollard was a "stiff." Pollard then rushed for 99 yards and two touchdowns and caught four passes for another 48 yards as the Steelers upset the Broncos, 24-17, in Mile High Stadium.

•

13 Chuck Noll attended Marshall Law School at night for three years while he was playing for the Cleveland Browns in the 1950s.

•

14 Quarterback Cliff Stoudt earned two Super Bowl rings and qualified for his NFL pension before he ever played in a game. Stoudt, the Steelers' fifth-round draft choice from Youngstown State in 1977, made the team but did not get in a game for three seasons, until 1980, when he played in six of them.

•

15 For years, one of the biggest Steelers' secrets was the salary of Coach Chuck Noll. Then, in 1990, a court order required NFL teams to release some financial information for an anti-trust suit in Minneapolis. The Steelers' books showed that Noll earned $717,000 in 1990. After his retirement in 1991, the Steelers paid him a $1 million annuity over the next 10 years.

MORE NICKNAMES

Match the Steeler with his nickname.

1 Francis Kilroy
2 Tom Tracy
3 John Henry Johnson
4 Garry Howe
5 Jim Brandt
6 Edgar Maske
7 Jack Deloplaine
8 Jack McClairen
9 Dick Campbell
10 Paul Younger

a) Goose
b) Stumpy
c) Tank
d) Hydroplane
e) Bucko
f) Soup
g) The Bomb
h) Mumbles
i) Eggs
j) Popcorn

ANSWERS: 1-e, 2-g, 3-h, 4-b, 5-j, 6-i, 7-d, 8-a, 9-f, 10-c.

Rushers
Word Search

Find the Steelers' number one rushers (1941–1993).

NAMES	*YEARS*
RIFFLE	1941
DUDLEY	1942, 1946
HINKLE	1943
GRIGAS	1944
WARREN	1945
CLEMENT	1947
CIFERS	1948
NUZUM	1949
GERI	1950
ROGEL	1951, 1953–56
MATHEWS	1952
WELLS	1957
TRACY	1958–60
JOHNSON	1961–64
HOAK	1965, 1968–69
ASBURY	1966
SHY	1967
FUQUA	1970–71
HARRIS	1972–83
POLLARD	1984–85
JACKSON	1986–87
HOGE	1988, 1990–91
WORLEY	1989
FOSTER	1992
THOMPSON	1993

```
X B C V S L L E W L S M R N R S I B C L F B
Z Q G K H A L Q V J A T V A U R W E A M Q M
E Y V D Z F Y N I L G Q M P E O T B O A L T
G A P K F E D H P R I S U G R S P C L T Y O
R N B I W O T B O I R J T A Y W H E S H V U
I O R V E L H W L E G O R Z E M Z V S E K Z
O S U L C Q O P L T R L S J O R K Q B W U J
P N K K B V M M A S B U R Y P R T L W S I O
A H A F P D P X R O K P E O R A S A R F T L
W O R L E Y S G D F S M O T D C I F E R S T
H J V I O H O C N M Z K C D N J W O G V U S
H W G N T U N R U A U Q U F Q B A W X R T N
A C P M B H L Z S V D E O N H K R M F Y H B
D E U G Q F U A H U G Y A L P N R S P O V N
M G C I T N E M E L C C J U E T E G J H I O
V O F K J C S G H A R R I S L R N P W F R S
A H L Y N F D T R S L L O E K S L S M B V K
N P S O X J U T V R W D M S N W R I Y L K C
O W I S R N Y V F O S T E R I F U V M H R A
Y E L D U D V L P C L O V S H N O S G X O J
```

WHO AM I?

1 I became the first big-money player in the NFL when the Steelers paid me $15,800 to play in 1938. I retired from football, studied law, and eventually went into government work. Who am I?

•

2 I was born in South Africa. My father was a pro soccer player in England. I became a United States citizen in June 1985. Who am I?

•

3 I was one of the few black quarterbacks in the NFL in the early 1970s. My father was a college football head coach. I crossed the players' picket line during the 1974 strike and opened the season as the starting quarterback. Who am I?

•

4 I was a quarterback for the Steelers in the 1950s and later became an executive with the Minnesota Vikings, Chicago Bears, New Orleans Saints, and baseball's Chicago Cubs. I was nearly elected NFL Commissioner in 1989. Who am I?

•

5 Mel Blount broke my team interception record. I was picked to the all-NFL team of the decades at cornerback, although I also played safety. I now head the NFL's Blesto Scouting Combine, based in Pittsburgh. Who am I?

•

6 I was the Steelers' leading receiver in 1968 and 1969 but when Chuck Noll thought I had challenged him, he traded me to Baltimore in 1970 for wide receiver Willie Richardson, along with a draft choice. Who am I?

•

7 I was the first rookie running back to lead the Steelers in rushing since Franco Harris in 1972. I was later traded to the Chicago Bears. Who am I?

•

8 I was a free-agent rookie in 1974, the year the Steelers had one of the best drafts in NFL history. I made the ballclub as a special teams performer, later became a starter, earned four Super Bowl rings, and intercepted 51 passes before I retired after 14 seasons in Pittsburgh. Who am I?

•

9 I was a running back drafted by the Steelers on the second round in 1953, but spurned their offer and played for Calgary in the CFL. They traded my rights to San Francisco for back Ed Fullerton. I played for the 49ers and Detroit Lions before finally joining the Steelers in 1960, seven years after they drafted me. I spent six seasons with them and am now in the Hall of Fame. Who am I?

•

10 I played at Pitt and was the Steelers' first-round draft choice in 1964. I tied for the team interception lead in 1968 and 1969. I later earned my law degree and was president of both the Pittsburgh Maulers and the Pittsburgh Penguins. I also helped settle the 1982 NFL players' strike. Who am I?

ANSWERS TO WHO AM I?

1 Halfback Byron White, who retired in 1993 after serving 31 years as a justice of the United States Supreme Court.

2 Placekicker Gary Anderson.

3 Joe Gilliam.

4 Jim Finks.

5 Jack Butler.

6 Roy Jefferson.

7 Tim Worley.

8 Strong safety Donnie Shell.

9 John Henry Johnson.

10 Paul Martha.

FOURTH QUARTER

50 QUESTIONS

1 Name the school Steelers founder Art Rooney did NOT attend.

a) Slippery Rock
b) Indiana University of Pennsylvania
c) Duquesne
d) Georgetown

•

2 Name the three Louisiana natives who started at quarterback for the Steelers in the 1980s.

•

3 In 1983, wide receiver Jim Smith jumped to the USFL and a year later quarterback Cliff Stoudt joined him. Which USFL team did these Steelers join?

•

4 Of the 22 Steelers who played on all four Super Bowl teams, only two were waived by them. Can you name both?

a) Randy Grossman
b) Dwight White
c) Franco Harris
d) Larry Brown
e) L. C. Greenwood

•

5 Which two of those 22 four-time Super Bowl players were traded to another team?

a) Franco Harris
b) J. T. Thomas
c) Steve Furness
d) Mike Webster
e) Randy Grossman

•

6 Which of those 22 four-time Super Bowl players was the last one to play for the Steelers?

•

7 True or False: Jim Thorpe once played for the Steelers.

•

8 Which of these Pro Football Hall of Famers DID NOT play for the Steelers?

a) Marion Motley
b) Cal Hubbard
c) Bert Bell
d) Len Dawson
e) Bill Hewitt

•

9 Three players named Bradshaw wore Steelers uniforms. Name them. BONUS: List their positions.

•

10 Who led the Steelers in rushing in 1967? (Hint: No one has led them with fewer yards between 1952 and now.)

•

11 What was the headline in the *Pittsburgh Post-Gazette* the day after the Steelers lost their 1989 opener to Cleveland, 51-0?

a) "Noll Must Go!"
b) "51-0!"
c) "Mulligan!"
d) "O-My!"

•

12 True or False: Roy Gerela never made a field goal from 50 yards or longer.

•

13 Which of these players never made the Pro Bowl?

a) Sam Davis
b) David Little
c) Larry Brown
d) Earnest Jackson

•

14 Name the Steelers quarterback who has thrown for the second-most yardage in their history?

•

15 Hall of Fame linebacker Jack Ham and guard Carlton Haselrig come from this western Pennsylvania town.

•

16 True or False: Pittsburgh had just one pro football team in the 1930s.

•

17 Which one of the following reasons did Bill Cowher cite for his team's success in 1992?

a) The four Super Bowl trophies in the Steelers' lobby
b) Great coaching
c) An easy schedule
d) Pittsburgh newspaper strike

•

18 True or False: Former Boston Celtics star John Havlicek once played football against the Steelers.

•

19 Which Steeler slapped his hand on the turf three times to count out Al Toon, after the New York Jets' wide receiver was knocked out in a 1989 game?

•

20 Who was MVP of the Super Bowl IX victory over Minnesota?

•

21 Which team signed quarterback Neil O'Donnell to an offer sheet in 1992, prompting the Steelers to match it seven days later?

•

22 Who was the first Steeler to rush for 1,000 yards?

•

23 Who was the first Steeler to combine for 2,000 yards rushing and receiving?

•

24 Name a running back who had a better career average per carry than Franco Harris.

a) Fran Rogel
b) Frank Pollard
c) Dick Hoak
d) Tom Tracy

•

25 What did Coach Buddy Parker get in return when he traded Buddy Dial to Dallas in 1964?

a) A first-round draft pick
b) 24 cases of Lone Star beer
c) Nothing
d) $50,000
e) An ulcer

•

26 Who holds the Steelers' record for most yards receiving in one season?

a) Buddy Dial
b) John Stallworth
c) Lynn Swann
d) Louis Lipps

•

27 Who was the only Steeler named to the NFL–AFL 25-Year All-Star Team?

•

28 Who presented Art Rooney Sr. when he was inducted into the Hall of Fame in 1964?

•

29 Name the three future Hall of Famers who played their last season with the Steelers in 1983.

•

30 In 1970 the Steelers acquired running back Frenchy Fuqua and linebacker Henry Davis from the New York Giants. What did the Giants get in return?

a) A third-round draft pick
b) Chuck Noll's eternal gratitude
c) Nothing
d) Quarterback Dick Shiner

•

31 Why didn't the Steelers have a third-round draft pick in 1979?

a) They waited too long to choose and the clock ran out
b) In the interest of NFL parity, they passed
c) They traded it
d) The NFL took it from them because they illegally wore shoulder pads during minicamp in 1978

•

32 Who is the only player to win the Steelers' MVP award three times?

a) Rod Woodson
b) Jack Lambert
c) Terry Bradshaw
d) John Henry Johnson

•

33 Which two players were in the same backfield of Notre Dame in the 1960s and the Steelers in the 1970s?

•

34 What season did the Steelers switch from the 4-3 defense with four down linemen to the 3-4 with only three linemen?

•

35 How many times did the Steelers lose to the Cleveland Browns in Three Rivers Stadium between 1970 and 1985?

•

36 Terry Bradshaw threw five touchdown passes against Atlanta on November 15, 1981. Which other quarterback has thrown five TD passes in a game?

a) Bubby Brister
b) Mark Malone
c) Cliff Stoudt
d) Jim Finks

•

37 Name the only Steeler selected to the NFL's All-1930s team.

•

38 When did Pittsburgh have its first winning record?

•

39 How many times did Chuck Noll's team win an NFL championship?

•

40 True or False: Actor Ed O'Neill, who plays Al Bundy on TV's "Married with Children," played for the Steelers.

•

41 What year did Art Rooney relinquish the title of Steelers president to his son, Dan?

•

42 Which Pittsburgh sportswriter did Joe Greene spit on in 1970?

a) Jack Sell
b) Pat Livingston
c) Al Abrams
d) Phil Musick
e) John Clayton

•

43 Who recovered the onside kick with 17 seconds left to preserve the Steelers' 35-31 victory over Dallas in Super Bowl XIII?

a) Lynn Swann
b) Tony Dungy
c) Rocky Bleier
d) Dennis Winston

•

44 What Hall of Fame running back did the Steelers bypass in the first round of the 1957 draft?

•

45 What Hall of Fame quarterback did the Steelers pick in the first round of the 1957 draft?

•

46 Who is the only Steeler other than Franco Harris to rush for 100 yards in two straight post-season games?

•

47 Which Steeler assistant coach did not take a job as a head coach in the USFL?

a) Woody Widenhofer
b) Bud Carson
c) George Perles
d) Rollie Dotsch

•

48 True or False: Franco Harris scored all four of the Steelers' rushing TDs in their four Super Bowls.

•

49 How many times did Terry Bradshaw throw for 400 yards in a game?

•

50 Who is the only Steelers quarterback in the NFL's all-time list of top 20 passers based on their efficiency rating?

ANSWERS TO 50 QUESTIONS

1 a) Slippery Rock.

2 Terry Bradshaw, David Woodley, Bubby Brister.

3 The Birmingham Stallions.

4 c and e. (Harris was cut after he held out during the 1984 training camp, and L. C. Greenwood was waived during 1982 training camp.)

5 b and c.

6 Center Mike Webster, 1988

7 False. Thorpe's NFL career, which began in 1915 with the Canton Bulldogs, ended with the Chicago Cardinals in 1928, five years before Pittsburgh entered the league.

8 c) Bell was a co-owner of the club but never played.

9 Charley Bradshaw, offensive tackle (1961–66); Jim Bradshaw, back (1963–67); Terry Bradshaw, quarterback (1970–83).

10 Don Shy, 341 yards on 99 carries.

11 b.

12 True.

13 a) Although Davis is regarded as the best guard in Steelers history.

14 Bubby Brister, 10,104 yards.

15 Johnstown.

16 False. The Pittsburgh Americans of the old AFL competed in 1936 and 1937.

17 d.

18 True. On August 18, 1962, Havlicek, a rookie split end in the Cleveland Browns' training camp, threw a block that helped spring Jim Brown on a 45-yard run in an exhibition game against the Steelers. Four days later, the Browns cut Havlicek, who appealed to another court.

19 Linebacker Greg Lloyd.

20 Franco Harris.

21 Tampa Bay.

22 John Henry Johnson, 1,141 yards in 1962.

23 Barry Foster, 2,034 yards in 1992.

24 b) Frank Pollard, 4.2 yards per carry (Harris had 4.1).

25 c) Dallas traded the Steelers the draft rights to Scott Appleton, who signed with Houston of the AFL instead.

26 b) Stallworth, 1,395 yards in 1984.

27 Linebacker Jack Lambert.

28 David Lawrence, former governor of Pennsylvania and Pittsburgh mayor.

29 Mel Blount, Terry Bradshaw, Franco Harris.

30 d.

31 d.

32 a) 1990, 1993, and co-winner in 1988.

33 Halfback Rocky Bleier and quarterback Terry Hanratty.

34 1982.

35 None; they won 16 in a row before losing 27-24 in 1986 at home.

36 b) Against Indianapolis on September 8, 1985.

37 Back Johnny (Blood) McNally.

38 1942, 7-4 (2nd in Eastern Division).

39 Seven. He coached four Super Bowl champs with the Steelers, played on two NFL champions with the Cleveland Browns, and was an assistant coach with the Baltimore Colts when they won the NFL title in 1968 but lost the pre-merger Super Bowl to the New York Jets.

40 False. But he *was* a rookie linebacker in their training camp in 1969. Bundy—er, O'Neill—was a six-foot-three, 230-pound free agent from Youngstown State. But Chuck Noll, a rookie coach that year, yelled CUT! That ended O'Neill's football career.

41 1975.

42 b) Livingston of the *Pittsburgh Press.*

43 c) Bleier.

44 Jim Brown.

45 Len Dawson.

46 Merril Hoge, 100 yards vs. Houston on December 31, 1992 and 120 yards vs. Denver on January 7, 1993.

47 b) Carson (Widenhofer-Oklahoma, Perles-Philadelphia, Dotsch-Birmingham).

48 True.

49 None.

50 Len Dawson, who spent his first three pro seasons (1957–59) with the Steelers as a backup, and then went on to play 16 more years in the AFL and NFL.

The 1943 Steagles

WAR STORIES—WHERE STEAGLES FLY

What did you do in the war, Daddy?

Son, I was a Steagle.

A *Steagle?*

Well, the official name was the Philadelphia-Pittsburgh Eagles. A sportswriter dubbed them the Steagles and it stuck, thank goodness.

This was 1943, the middle of World War II and the NFL had trouble fielding teams, as you can imagine. The Cleveland Rams closed up shop for the remainder of the war, reducing the number of NFL teams to nine. In order to survive, the franchises in Philadelphia and Pittsburgh merged for one year, 1943, to compete as the Steagles.

Teams back then found players wherever they could—men classified 4F for various reasons, college students, those too old to fight but not too old to block or tackle. The War Department also permitted soldiers to leave their duty in the fall in order to play football and then return to duty when the season ended. Rosters were reduced from 33 to 28 men.

The Steagles had co-coaches. Philadelphia's Earl "Greasy" Neale coached the offense and Pittsburgh's Walt Kiesling ran the defense. Both were destined for the Pro Football Hall of Fame. The team practiced in Philadelphia and played four home games at Shibe Park in Philly and two at Forbes Field in Pittsburgh. They practiced at night because most of them worked in defense factories by day. Some players worked in other cities and either did not practice or practiced only on occasion. Frank "Bucko" Kilroy, for example, was stationed at a reserve school in New York City and made practice once a week.

The team's quarterback was Roy Zimmerman, who completed just 43 of 124 passes and threw 17 interceptions and only nine touchdowns. Jack Hinkle led the Steagles with 571 yards rushing and Tony Bova led them with 17 pass receptions for 419 yards.

Ernie Steele and Bob Thurbon each scored six touchdowns. Tackle Victor Sears, an original Eagle, was the only Steagle to make All-Pro.

The Steagles weren't a bad ball club. They opened the season with victories over Brooklyn and New York, both in Philadelphia. The Steagles then landed, losing big on the road to the Chicago Bears and New York Giants. They rebounded to go 5-3-1, beating first-place Washington, 27-14, on the road on November 28. That set up a season-ending game against Green Bay in Philadelphia on December 5, with a chance for the Steagles to tie for the Eastern Division crown with the Giants and Washington. But before 34,294 at Shibe Park, the Packers beat the Steagles, 38-28, and Phil-Pitt finished its only season 5-4-1.

On that day, December 5, 1943, the merger of the two franchises automatically dissolved.

Pittsburgh merged with the Chicago Cardinals in 1944 and the team was known as the Card-Pitts, who went 0-10 and were derisively called the "Carpets." Fullback Johnny Griggs rushed for 610 yards, second in the NFL, but quit in disgust before the last game. The Card-Pitts were outscored, 328-108.

The Eagles resumed play under their original banner. They went on to play their old mates in a divisional playoff in 1947 after they tied for first place in the Eastern Division at 8-4. Philadelphia beat visiting Pittsburgh, 21-0, after the Steelers staged a one-day walk-out during the week because they wanted more money. The Eagles lost the title game to the Chicago Cardinals the following week, 28-21.

But Philadelphia won NFL titles under Neale in each of the next two seasons, 1948 and 1949. Philadelphia won another NFL championship in 1960. The Steelers? They did not appear in another championship playoff game until 1972, then won four Super Bowls in the 1970s.

COLLEGE MATCH 'EM UP

Pair the player with his alma mater.

1 Mike Webster
2 Elbie Nickel
3 David Little
4 Lynn Swann
5 Jack Ham
6 Donnie Shell
7 Walt Kiesling
8 Rocky Bleier
9 Roy Gerela
10 Terry Bradshaw
11 Ernie Stautner
12 Johnny McNally
13 Mike Wagner
14 Ron Shanklin
15 Jim Smith
16 Dick Leftridge
17 Jack Lambert
18 Dermontti Dawson
19 Greg Lloyd
20 Louis Lipps

a) Boston College
b) Cincinnati
c) Wisconsin
d) New Mexico State
e) Notre Dame
f) Florida
g) St. Thomas
h) Southern Cal
i) Louisiana Tech
j) Penn State
k) St. John (Minn.)
l) South Carolina State
m) West Virginia
n) Kentucky
o) Kent State
p) Fort Valley State
q) Western Illinois
r) Southern Mississippi
s) Michigan
t) North Texas State

ANSWERS: 1-c, 2-b, 3-f, 4-h, 5-j, 6-l, 7-g, 8-e, 9-d, 10-i, 11-a, 12-k, 13-q, 14-t, 15-s, 16-m, 17-o, 18-n, 19-p, 20-r.

Steelers of the 1930s
Word Search

Find the Steelers of the 1930s.

NAME	*YEARS*
DOUDS (Forrest)	1933–35
GENTRY (Byron)	1937–39
HELLER (Warren)	1934–36
KARCIS (John)	1936–38
LEVEY (Jim)	1934–36
MAYHEW (Hayden)	1936–38
McNALLY (Johnny)	1934, 1937–39
NICCOLAI (Armand)	1934–42
RADO (George)	1935–37
SANDBERG (Sigurd)	1935–37
SORTET (Wilbur)	1933–40
SNYDER (Bill)	1934–35
GILDEA (John)	1935–37

```
S B E J K J L T M B M N A M I S S I M
O N W O F U Y N B T E B Y E V E L Q G
S C X D Z I V S A M R H G D L P E I K
A U J Q D J A N I C C O L A I X N E A
N D V O S O K P I W G M P R Y M S Z B
D A L Q Z J U H T N F X C V R J N E G
B T P F U O Y D I D S L A H W B Y U S
E L O N K M W D S V K E A Z R H D E Q
R U F J I M X C Z S D P B G Y W E N J
G P T I H R A D E L H Y Q M X F R L V
B A I D E Q U O I G G Y S N W F K J E
Y T N Z L H V G T W C G R P L X R B U
F H D B L S X M V G E N T R Y K O Z Q
C Z W S E G M T K C Q I A V S O E T W
L R J A R L E D P J F Y U I H N B X E
E C N U G T P M W R K E C A O Y S I H
G V Q I R N F B T Z P R K J H D X L Y
U N Y O W M S J I O A H G A O K Q L A
B M S T M R G E V K K P Y L L A N C M
L C X L R F B V P J H T H D I N E Z F
Q N K W A U R A D O G D J M Y P S R O
```

ANOTHER NUMBERS GAME

Part I

Here are the numbers: 10, 20, 22, 35, 38, 42, 56, 57, 76, 82, 83, 87, 99. Match them with the players who wore them.

______ Whizzer White
______ Darryl Sims
______ Paul Martha
______ John Stallworth
______ Bobby Layne
______ Dick Hoak
______ John Henry Johnson
______ Roy Jefferson
______ Gene Lipscomb
______ Mike Merriweather
______ Robin Cole
______ Louis Lipps
______ Tim Worley

Part II

1 Tony Parisi, the Steelers' longtime equipment man, has refused to reissue some of the most revered numbers in the team's history to new players. Since their retirement the following players' numbers have never been worn by anyone else. Can you list their numbers?

Terry Bradshaw ______
Franco Harris ______
Mike Webster ______
Jack Lambert ______
Ernie Stautner ______

Joe Greene ______
Donnie Shell ______

2 Parisi did issue Hall of Famer Jack Ham's number to little-known linebacker Todd Seabaugh. He wore it for one season, 1984, and Parisi has put it in mothballs since. That number is ______

3 Conversely, because NFL rules limit most wide receivers to numbers in the 80s, Parisi has reissued Lynn Swann's number at least eight times since his retirement after the 1982 season. Since then, Swann's number has been worn by some of the most obscure receivers in Steelers history: Craig Dunaway (1983), John Rodgers (1984), Jessie Britt (1986), Joey Clinkscales (1987–88), Jason Johnson (1989), Chris Calloway (1990–91), Mark Diddio (1992), and Andre Hastings (1993). Swann's number was ______

4 Joe Greene wore this number as a rookie during part of the exhibition season in 1969 and never wore it after that ______

Part III

1 In the 1970s this sign hung in Three Rivers Stadium: "12 + 88 = 6." What did it mean?

2 What did Bubby Brister say when he was issued the number 6?

a) "That's an upside-down 9, you know."

b) "I'm number 6, write it down."

c) "Sex?"

d) "I'll be happy if I'm half the quarterback Terry Bradshaw [number 12] was."

3 How many players have worn the number 13 for the Steelers in a game?

4 Who was the only player to wear number 0?

5 What other players besides kicker Gary Anderson have worn the number 1?

6 How many players wore the number 99 from 1933 through 1984?

Answers to Part I

White, 10; Sims, 99; Martha, 20; Stallworth, 82; Layne, 22; Hoak, 42; Johnson, 35; Jefferson, 87; Lipscomb, 76; Merriweather, 57; Cole, 56; Lipps, 83; Worley, 38.

Answers to Part II

1. Bradshaw, 12; Harris, 32; Webster, 52; Lambert, 58; Stautner, 70, Greene, 75; Shell, 31.

2. 59.

3. 88.

4. 72.

Answers to Part III

1. Terry Bradshaw to Lynn Swann = Touchdown.

2. d.

3. Two. Quarterback Bill Mackrides in 1953 and center Lee Mulleneaux in 1936.

4. Jack Collins, 1952, but he never got into a game.

5. Dave Trout (1981), Merlyn Condit (1940), Warren Heller (1936).

6. None.

Greg Lloyd

YOU CAN SAY THAT AGAIN

The Steelers, desperate for a running back, signed serviceable Earnest Jackson off waivers from Philadelphia early in the 1986 season. As reporters feverishly made phone calls and tapped out their stories in the press room, Art Rooney Sr. wandered in practically unnoticed. He looked around, bemused at the hubbub, and said:

"You know, this guy isn't Gale Sayers we just signed."

•

The recently hired Chuck Noll, when asked how he would win in Pittsburgh:

"Whatever it takes."

•

Quarterback Bubby Brister, after he refused Joe Walton's orders to replace Neil O'Donnell late in a 31-6 loss at Houston in 1991:

"I'm no . . . relief quarterback. I don't mop up for anybody."

•

Linebacker Greg Lloyd, after NBC's Joe Namath criticized his style of play in 1991:

"Who is Joe Namath? This is a guy who, if he played in the league today, I'd probably just go hit him late and see what he did, just for the hell of it. Joe Namath can go to hell; he can kiss Greg's ass."

•

Broadcaster Myron Cope, introducing Chuck Noll at a Pittsburgh rally after the Steelers won their fourth Super Bowl:

"All hail the Emperor Chaz!"

•

Rookie linebacker Jack Lambert, when Steeler veterans tried to make him sing the fight song to his alma mater, Kent State, at training camp in 1974:

"I'm not singing anything."

•

Barry Foster

Chuck Noll, when asked a question about Franco Harris during his celebrated 1984 training camp holdout:

"Franco Who?"

•

Running back Preston Pearson on the Steelers' quarterback situation in 1974:

"If Terry Hanratty had Brad's body, or Brad had Hanratty's head, we'd have one helluva quarterback."

•

Dr. John Baughman to Rocky Bleier in 1969, shortly after Bleier's right foot was severely damaged by a grenade in Vietnam:

"Rocky, you won't be able to play again. It's impossible."

•

Barry Foster, following his record-breaking 1992 season in which he led the AFC with 1,690 yards rushing and was named the Steelers' MVP:

"Money talks and everything else walks."